QUARKXPRESS
in easy steps

Robert Shufflebotham

COMPUTER STEP

In easy steps is an imprint of Computer Step
Southfield Road . Southam
Warwickshire CV33 OFB . England

Tel: 01926 817999 Fax: 01926 817005
http://www.computerstep.com

Notice of Liability
Every effort has been made to ensure that this book contains accurate
and current information. However, Computer Step and the author shall
not be liable for any loss or damage suffered by readers as a result of
any information contained herein.

Trademarks
All trademarks are acknowledged as belonging to their respective
companies.

Printed and bound in the United Kingdom

ISBN 1-874029-99-7

Contents

The Working Environment

QuarkXPress is a powerful, sophisticated page layout application capable of producing anything from a simple, single-sided leaflet through to complex magazine or newspaper layouts as well as longer publications such as manuals and books.

This chapter gets you started using QuarkXPress, introducing you to the working environment, document setup, and useful conventions and techniques that will prove invaluable as you build your QuarkXPress skills.

Covers

Chapter One

Document Setup

HANDY TIP

When a dialogue box is active, press the tab key on your keyboard to move the highlight from entry field to entry field. This is a standard technique you can use in all Macintosh and Windows dialogue boxes. Once an entry field is highlighted just type the numbers you want on the keyboard. The highlighted value is replaced by whatever you type. Use the arrow keys and the delete key to correct any mistakes you make in an entry field.

Once you have launched QuarkXPress and the copyright screen appears along with the XPress menu bar and Tool palette, you can proceed to set up a new document.

Size and Orientation

1 To create a new document, choose File > New. From the sub-menu choose Document. Use the Size pop-up menu to choose a standard, predefined page size if appropriate.

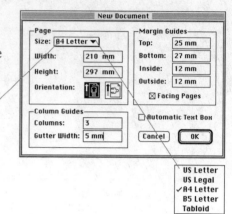

2 To create a non-standard page size, make sure the Width entry field is highlighted, then enter the page width you require. Then, either double-click on the Height entry field, or press and drag across it with your cursor to highlight the existing value. Enter a new value for the height.

3 The default orientation is portrait. Click the landscape icon if you want a landscape page.

Margin Guides

Use the Margin guides section of the New Document dialogue box to create non-printing margin guides and also to specify whether your publication is to use facing pages or not. Margin guides appear as blue lines on your page.

HANDY TIP

The maximum page size is 48x48 inches. The minimum is 1x1 inch.

Enter values in the margin guides entry boxes to specify the sizes of your margins. Margins indicate the main text area of your page. But, you are not constrained to working within the margins you set – picture boxes, text boxes and lines can sit outside the margin area, or even cross the margins.

2   Click Facing Pages if you want to set up a double-sided document such as a multi-page brochure, a magazine or book, where you will be working with double-page spreads. Leave the Facing Pages option deselected if you are setting up a document that will be printed single-sided (on one side of the paper only).

Column Guides

Column guides appear on your screen in blue. They are non-printing and act as a grid that you work to. You are not constrained to working within the columns – picture boxes, text boxes and lines can span one or several columns giving you complete flexibility to create the page design you want.

1   Enter the number of columns you want. XPress automatically calculates the widths of the columns based on the number you specify, the width of any margins, the overall width of the page and the gutter width specified.

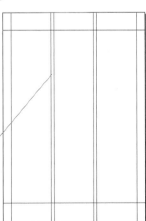

2   Enter a value in the Gutter width entry box. This defines the space between columns on your page.

Automatic Text Box

The Automatic Text Box option creates a document that automatically sets up a text box which conforms to the margin and column settings in the New Document dialogue box. If you have specified multiple columns the automatic text box is generated with the same number of columns and fits within the margins you define in Document Setup.

Select the Automatic Text Box option if the document you want to create has a predominantly regular, fixed page design. An Automatic Text Box would be useful in a novel, or a technical manual, where the text sits in the same text area, page after page after page.

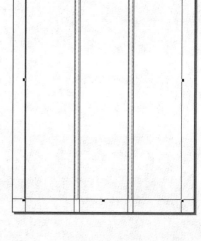

For most magazines, and design intensive brochures and leaflets, where the page layout varies from page to page, it is best to leave the Automatic Text Box option deselected.

When you import a text file into an Automatic Text Box, the text flows into the first page and if there is more text in the text file than will fit into the initial box, QuarkXPress automatically generates enough additional pages, with automatic boxes on them, until all the text has been placed.

Opening Documents

REMEMBER

QuarkXPress version 4 can open documents, templates and libraries created in version 2.1 or later. The document version of the file you select in the Open dialogue box is indicated near the bottom of the dialogue box.

BEWARE

You cannot open version 4 documents using earlier versions of QuarkXPress.

HANDY TIP

If you get the Non-matching Preferences dialogue box when you open an existing document, choose 'Keep Changes' to open the document with the settings saved in the original file. This helps ensure that line endings do not change due to text reflow.

As well as creating new documents using the New Document dialogue box, you can open an existing QuarkXPress document from the File menu.

1 To open an existing QuarkXPress version 3.3x or version 4 document choose File > Open. Use standard Macintosh or Windows dialogue boxes to navigate to the folder which holds

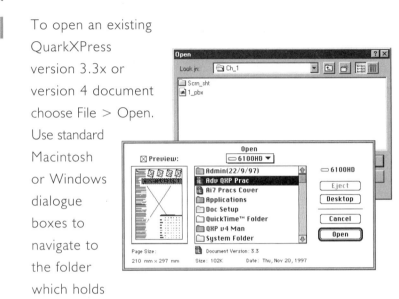

the file. Click on the file name to highlight it, then click the Open button. Or, double-click the file name.

2 In the Finder (Mac) or Windows environment, you can double-click a QuarkXPress version 4 icon to launch the application and open the file you double-click on.

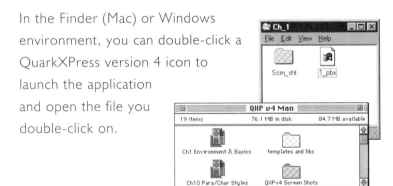

Mac and Windows Screens

Although the Macintosh and Windows environments have their own conventions and 'feel', the two are moving closer and closer together. Examine the screen shot of QuarkXPress on the Mac and under Windows, and you will see that the functionality of the application is virtually identical on both platforms. Once you know QuarkXPress on one platform, you know it on the other.

Choose View > Show/Hide Rulers to show or hide the Horizontal and Vertical rulers.

Click and drag on the title bar to reposition the QuarkXPress document window.

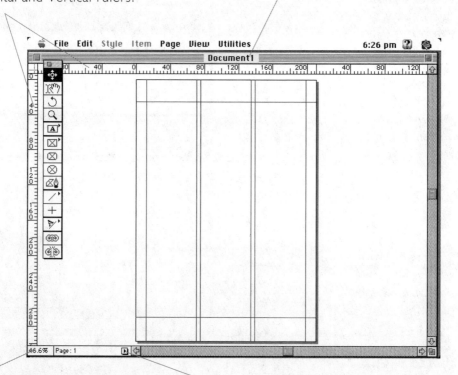

Double-click in the View Percent field, or drag across it, to highlight the View Percentage. Then enter a new value. Press Return/Enter to apply the new value.

Click and hold on the Page Indicator pop-up (if you have more than one page in the document) to access page number icons. Select a page icon to move to that page.

...cont'd

The majority of screen shots used in this book are taken from the Macintosh platform – the traditional home of QuarkXPress. Wherever possible, screen shots from the Windows platform have been used to allow comparison between platforms. These days, if you know QuarkXPress on one platform, it's safe to say, you know it on the other platform, and with computer technology changing constantly and rapidly, that can't be a bad thing.

The Pasteboard area surrounds the pages in your document. You can place items on the pasteboard, but only items on a page will print. Items on the pasteboard are saved as part of the XPress document.

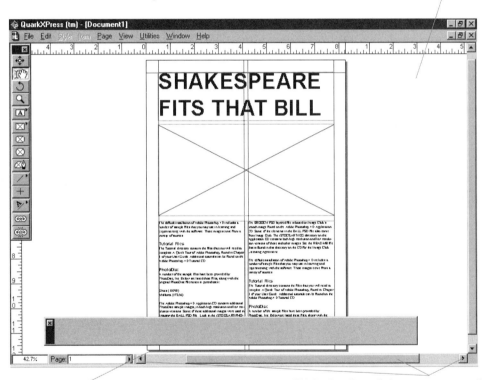

An A4 page in 'Fit in Window' view. The drop shadow to the right and bottom of the page is simply a visual aid, it does not print, but helps to visually define the edge of the page.

Click the Scroll Arrows to scroll the page in increments, drag the Scroll Box to move the page a custom amount, click on the Scroll Bar either side of the Scroll Box, to jump the page in half-screen increments.

The Tool Palette

There are a number of useful techniques and conventions that you can use when working with tools in the Tool Palette to improve your efficiency as you work with QuarkXPress.

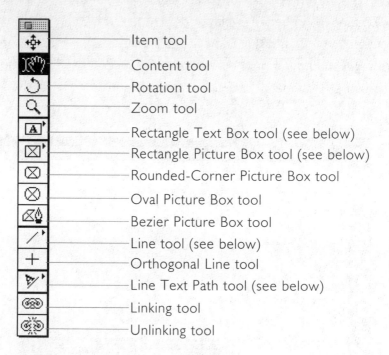

Item tool
Content tool
Rotation tool
Zoom tool
Rectangle Text Box tool (see below)
Rectangle Picture Box tool (see below)
Rounded-Corner Picture Box tool
Oval Picture Box tool
Bezier Picture Box tool
Line tool (see below)
Orthogonal Line tool
Line Text Path tool (see below)
Linking tool
Unlinking tool

Rounded-corner, Concave-corner, Bevelled-corner, Oval, Bezier, Freehand Bezier text box tools

Concave-corner, Bevelled-corner, Freehand Bezier picture box tools

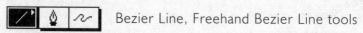

Bezier Line, Freehand Bezier Line tools

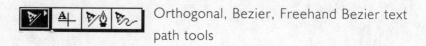

Orthogonal, Bezier, Freehand Bezier text path tools

...cont'd

1   To choose a tool, click once on the tool in the tool palette. Bring your cursor back onto the page. The cursor changes to reflect the tool you have chosen.

2   To cycle through the tools in the tool palette hold down Command (Mac), Crtl+Alt (Windows), then press the Tab key. You can cycle through the tools in reverse order by holding down Command+Shift (Mac), Ctrl+Alt+Shift (windows) and then pressing the Tab key.

3   A black pop-up triangle in a tool icon indicates that there are additional tools in that tool group. Press and hold on the tool to access the hidden tools. Once you have chosen one of the hidden tools, it remains displayed as the default tool in that group until you choose a different tool from the group.

 Do not keep the alt/option or Alt key depressed after you have clicked on a tool to select it. If you keep the key depressed when you bring the cursor back onto the page you activate the 'grabber hand' which is used to scroll the page.

4   Hold down alt/option (Mac), Alt (Windows), then click a drawing tool in the tool palette to prevent the tool selection from reverting to the Item or Content tool after you have drawn an item. Use this technique when you want to draw several picture boxes or text boxes of the same type without having to reselect the tool for each box.

5   Hold down Control (Mac), Ctrl (Windows) when you choose one of the hidden tools to add the tool to the main palette. The Tool palette grows to accommodate the new tool. To hide the tool again, hold down Control (Mac), Ctrl (Windows) and click on it once more.

Saving Documents

To avoid the possibility of losing work due to any kind of system failure or crash, you should do a Save As soon after starting work on a new document. Save (File > Save) regularly as you build the document.

Use File > Save As when you have created a new document. In the first instance use Save As to specify where you want to save the file on your hard disk, and to give it a name. Use standard Macintosh/ Windows dialogue boxes to navigate to appropriate folders or directories. You can also use the Save As command when you

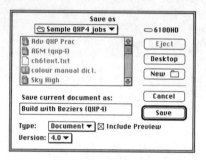

want to save a copy of the document you are working on. Immediately after using Save As in this way you continue working with a copy of the original document. The original remains at the stage at which it was last saved and in its original location.

HANDY TIP

The Revert to Saved Command (File > Revert to Saved) allows you to go back to the state of your document when you last saved, discarding all the changes you've made since you last saved.

2 Highlight the Save Current Document as entry field. Type in a name for the document, then click the Save button.

3 As you work in either a new XPress document that you created using File > New Document, or an existing document you have opened, you should save changes you make regularly using File > Save. This command simply updates the file with changes you have made since it was last saved. In the event of any kind of system crash or failure, you will be able to restart your system and continue working on the document from the point at which it was last saved.

...cont'd

 See page 23 for information on using the Autosave preference.

4 When you are working in QuarkXPress version 4 you can use the Version pop-up to choose from version 3.3 or version 4 format.

Version:	3.3
	✓ 4.0

If you choose version 3.3 format the document can be opened by QuarkXPress versions 3.3, 3.31 and 3.32. However, features specific to version 4 will be altered or removed.

5 When you open a v3.3x file in version 4 and first use File > Save, the Save As dialogue box appears. You can now choose whether to continue saving the file in v3.3 format or you can update it to version 4 format.

Templates should contain standard Master Page settings and elements, and all essential style sheets, colours, H&Js etc that you want to use repeatedly in future versions of the document.

6 Use the Type pop-up to save the document as a normal document, or as a template. Choose Template when you have created a standard layout that you want to use again without having to recreate all the standard elements. When you open a template, you actually open a copy of the file, leaving the original untouched. In this way the template remains intact and evey time you open it you get consistent results.

7 Select the Include Preview option if you want to see a thumbnail preview of the first page of the document in the Open dialogue box.

Type: ✓ Document / Template ☒ Include Preview

Open
☒ Preview: 6100HD ▼
Admin(22/9/97)
Adv QHP Prac
Ai7 Pracs Cover
Applications
Doc Setup
QuickTime™ Folder
QHP v4 Man
System Folder
Page Size:
210 mm × 297 mm
Document Version: 3.3
Size: 102K   Date: Thu, Nov 20, 1997
6100HD
Eject
Desktop
Cancel
Open

8 Click the Save button when you are satisfied.

Ruler Guides

To work with Snap to Guides, make sure that Snap to Guides in the View menu has a tick mark next to it, indicating that it is on.

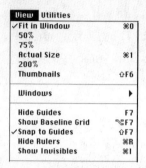

Like margin and column guides, ruler guides are non-printing guides that you can use for aligning items accurately. The default colour for ruler guides is green.

When Snap to Guides is on, your drawing tool cursors will lock onto guides when it comes within 6 screen pixels of the guide. This is useful when you are creating picture and text boxes and lines that must align precisely.

Also, when you move items, the edges of an item will snap onto guides.

I To create a ruler guide, make sure the rulers are showing. Choose View > Show Rulers if they are not. Position your cursor in either the top or left ruler, then press and drag onto the page area. Release the mouse button. If you are working with double-page spreads, this technique creates a guide that is specific to the page on which you release.

2 To reposition a ruler guide, select the Item tool, position your cursor on the guide, then press and drag. A double-headed

...cont'd

 You can reposition a guide using the Content tool, but only if there are no items below the cursor when you start to press and drag.

arrow cursor appears, indicating that you have picked up the guide.

3 To remove a ruler guide, drag it all the way back into the ruler it came from.

4 To create a ruler guide that spans both pages in a spread, drag from a ruler, but release when your cursor is on the pasteboard area (in other words, not on the page). The guide will run across the pasteboard and the pages in the spread.

5 To position a guide with numerical accuracy, make sure the measurements palette is showing (View > Show Measurements). As you drag a guide onto the page, you will see a read-out in the Measurements palette, indicating the precise position of the guide. Zoom in to have complete control over the positioning of the guide.

Zooming Techniques

Even if you have a large monitor, zooming in and out on areas of your page is a constant aspect of working in QuarkXPress.

1 Use the standard, preset views in the View menu to change the magnification of your page.

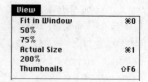

2 To zoom in on your page, click once on the Zoom tool in the Tool palette to select it. Position your cursor on the page, where you want to zoom in. Click the mouse button to zoom in using preset increments. (The default is 25%).

3 Alternatively, with the Zoom tool selected, you can press and drag to define an area of the page that you want to enlarge. The smaller the zoom box you draw, the greater the zoom amount.

4 To zoom back out, with the zoom tool selected, position your cursor on the page area, hold down alt/option (Mac), Alt (Windows). Notice the plus symbol in the centre of the zoom tool changes to a minus. Click to zoom out in the default preset increments.

5 To change the view using the View Percent Field, double-click the current value to highlight it,

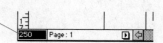

enter a new zoom value (from 10 – 800%), then press
Return/Enter. Alternatively, use the keyboard shortcut,
Control+V (Mac), Ctrl+Alt+V (Windows) to highlight the
field.

6   When you are working with any tool other than the Zoom
tool, you can temporarily access the Zoom tool by holding
down the Control key (Mac), Ctrl+Spacebar (Windows).
Make sure the cursor is positioned within the XPress
window. Click the mouse button, or press and drag to
zoom in. To access the Zoom out tool, hold down
Control+alt/option (Mac), Ctrl+Alt+Spacebar (Windows),
then click the mouse button.

7   (Windows) Click the right mouse button to display a
context sensitive pop-up menu. Choose from Fit in
Window, Actual Size and Thumbnails.

Document & Application Preferences

REMEMBER

A Default is a value or setting that XPress uses automatically in the first instance, until you set a different value.

Document Preferences

Document Preferences is a tabbed dialogue box with options for General, Paragraph, Character, Tool, and Trapping preferences. The dialogue box allows you to customise default preferences for the active QuarkXPress document.

1 To customise preferences for the active document, choose Edit > Preferences > Document. Click on a preference option tab, then make the changes you require.

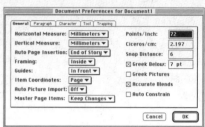

You will want to set up some settings just once (such as units of measure and some of the Tool preferences) – not every time you create a new document.

HANDY TIP

The principle of making changes to settings where there is no open document window also applies to changes you make to other specifications such as colours, style sheets, H&Js, lists and dashes and stripes.

2 To set a global default for the application (one that will apply to all documents you subsequently create), close down all XPress document windows until you have only the XPress menu bar and palettes visible.

3 Choose Edit > Preferences > Document (Command/ Ctrl+Y). Choose the settings you want for all subsequently created documents. Click OK in the dialogue box.

Application Preferences

The Application Preferences dialogue box is a tabbed dialogue box which allows you to create preferences that XPress will use for all documents.

One important Application Preference is the Auto Save option. When you specify an auto save interval of, for example 10 minutes, if your system does crash and you haven't saved recently, you will only lose up to the last 10 minutes work.

1   To switch on Auto Save, choose Edit > Preferences Application. Click the Save tab at the top of the dialogue box.

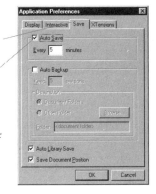

2   Click the Auto Save option, then enter a save interval – a number of minutes – to specify after what interval you want an auto save to take place.

When Auto Save is on, XPress automatically saves a temporary, auto-save file into the same folder/directory as the original file at the set intervals. This process does not overwrite the original file, but serves as a temporary backup. You overwrite the original file when you do a manual Save (File > Save).

When you open a document after a system crash you get a warning message indicating that the document will be restored to the last auto save version.

3   To revert to the last manually saved version of the document, choose File > Revert to Saved after you have opened the document.

In any case, you should get into the habit of saving your documents regularly, as you build them (File > Save). The Auto Save preference is a useful failsafe measure.

The Palettes

There are 9 floating palettes, including the Tool palette, in QuarkXPress which, when visible, always appear in front of the active document window. The palettes provide a convenient, visual and intuitive method of working in XPress, although there are alternative menu commands for achieving most of the options provided by the palettes.

This section uses Macintosh and Windows screen shots to indicate the identical functionality of the application on both platforms.

1   To show a palette, choose View menu, and then select the Show palette option for the palette you want.

2   To reposition a palette, position your cursor in the palette's title bar, then press and drag. A useful technique, if your screen is small, but you like to have various palettes available, is to position your palettes along the edge of the XPress window, so that the palette is only partially showing. When you want to use it, simply drag it back into the main window to make it fully visible.

3   Double-click the title bar of the palette to roll up the palette to a title bar only. Double-click the title bar again to reverse the procedure. (Macintosh) The WindowShade control panel must be switched on for this to work.

4   To close a palette, click the Close icon (Mac and Windows), or choose View menu and hide the appropriate palette.

5   Press and drag the palette's resize box (bottom right corner) to increase or decrease the size of the palette manually.

6   The Style Sheets and Document Layout Palettes have a divider bar that you can drag to resize the internal partitions of the palette.

7   In the Measurements palette, press and drag across a value, or double-click it to highlight it. Press the Tab key to move the highlight from entry field to entry field. Hold down Shift and press the Tab key to move backwards through the entry fields. Press Return/Enter to apply a change.

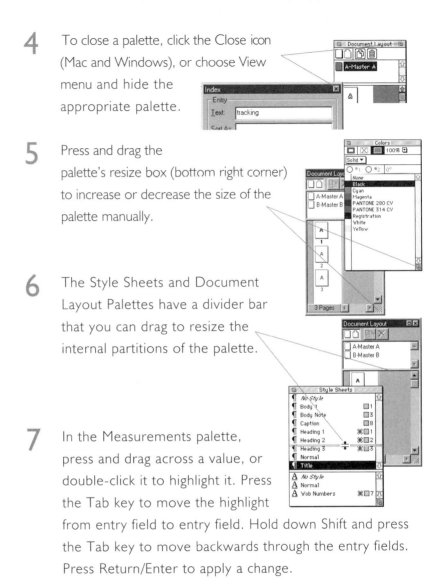

Scrolling

1 Use standard Macintosh/Windows techniques for scrolling the XPress page within the document window. Click the scroll arrows to move the page in increments; drag the scroll box to move the page in user-defined amounts; click the scroll bar between the scroll box and scroll arrows to jump the page in half screen increments.

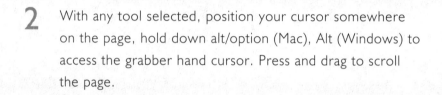

2 With any tool selected, position your cursor somewhere on the page, hold down alt/option (Mac), Alt (Windows) to access the grabber hand cursor. Press and drag to scroll the page.

Layout Basics

Items are the basic building blocks of all QuarkXPress pages. There are only three basic kinds of items – picture boxes, text boxes and lines – although each has many possible variations.

Use the techniques in this chapter to begin creating basic, single-page layouts.

Chapter Two

Covers

Drawing Standard Boxes

Boxes can contain text or pictures. They form the fundamental building blocks of all QuarkXPress pages. You can import or enter text into text boxes and you can import pictures into picture boxes.

Use the following techniques for all of the standard box drawing tools which include: the Rectangular, Rounded-corner, Concave-corner, Bevelled-corner, Oval Text Box drawing tools; the Rectangular, Concave-corner, Bevelled-corner Picture Box drawing tools; the Rounded-corner Picture Box drawing tool, the Oval Picture Box drawing tool.

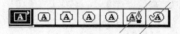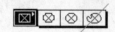

Not included are the Bezier box drawing tools. These are covered in Chapter 15.

1 To draw a box, select one of the standard text box or picture box drawing tools. Position your cursor on the page (the cursor changes to a drawing tool cursor), then press and drag away from the start point. Although you can press and drag in any direction, typically you will drag down and to the right.

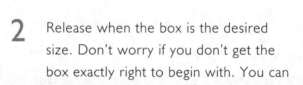

If you draw a really tiny box by mistake, it is easiest to delete it and start again. (See page 34).

2 Release when the box is the desired size. Don't worry if you don't get the box exactly right to begin with. You can always resize and reposition the box later.

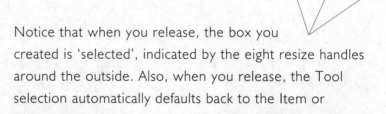

Notice that when you release, the box you created is 'selected', indicated by the eight resize handles around the outside. Also, when you release, the Tool selection automatically defaults back to the Item or Content tool, depending on which tool was last used.

Empty picture boxes are differen-tiated from text boxes by the cross running through the box. This is a non-printing guide and is only visible when Show Guides (View menu) is selected.

3 To draw a perfectly square or circular box, hold down the Shift key, then press and drag away from the start point.

...cont'd

HANDY TIP

If Snap to Guides is switched on (see page 18), your drawing cursor will snap onto the guide when it comes within 6 screen pixels of a column, margin or ruler guide. This is important when you want to draw boxes to fit exactly within these guides.

The Shift key acts as a constraint on the drawing tool. Make sure you release the mouse before you release the shift key, otherwise the constraint will be lost.

4 When you know that you want to create several boxes of the same type, hold down alt/option (Mac), Alt (Windows), then select a drawing tool. Once you have selected the drawing tool, release the alt/option or Alt key. You can now draw as many boxes as you want. (Holding down the alt/option key when you click on a tool prevents the tool selection from defaulting back to the Item or Content tool.) When you have finished drawing boxes, select any other tool to end the procedure.

Drawing and Modifying Lines

There are two basic line drawing tools – the Orthogonal Line drawing tool and the Line drawing tool.

1. To draw a horizontal or vertical line, click the Orthogonal Line drawing tool to select it. Position your cursor on the page, then press and drag to create the line. Release the mouse when the line is the length you want. Notice that the line is selected, indicated by the resize handle at each end, and that the tool selection reverts to either the Item or Content tool – depending on which was last used.

2. To draw a line at any angle, click on the Line tool to select it. Position your cursor on the page, then press and drag in any direction. Release when the line is the length you want. Hold down the Shift key, then press and drag with the Line tool to constrain the line to 45 degree increments. Remember to release the mouse button before you release the Shift key.

3. To modify a line, select it with either the Item or Content tool, then choose Item > Modify. Click the Line tab (see page 56 for further information on the options available for modifying lines.)

Moving Items Manually

BEWARE

Items placed on the pasteboard do not print, but they are saved as part of the document and therefore add to the file size. Items left on the pasteboard can also add to the processing time when you print.

HANDY TIP

When you have the Content tool selected and you want to move a picture or text box, instead of selecting the Item tool from the Tool palette, you can simply hold down Command/ Ctrl to gain temporary access to the Item tool. When you have moved the item and you release the Command/Ctrl key, the tool selection reverts to the Content tool.

You can move a box or a line anywhere on the page, or even onto the pasteboard area surrounding the page. Also, you can create 'bleeds' by positioning an item so that it runs across the edge of the page.

To create a bleed, make sure that the item you want to bleed off the edge of the page extends at least 3mm onto the pasteboard beyond the edge of the page.

1 To reposition items, select the Item tool. Position the cursor on the item you want to move. Press and drag to move the item to a new position. If you press then pause briefly before you drag, you can view the contents of the item as you move it.

2 To constrain the move horizontally or vertically, start to drag the item, then hold down the Shift key. Remember to release the mouse button, before you release the Shift key, otherwise the constraint effect of the Shift key will be lost.

3 To move an Item in one point increments, select the Item tool, click on an item to select it, then use the up, down, left or right arrow keys on the keyboard. You can move the item in 1/10th point increments by holding down the alt/option key (Mac), Alt (Windows) when using the arrow keys. Each time you use the key, the item moves an appropriate amount.

Selecting and Deselecting Items

Although their functions overlap to a certain extent, there is an important distinction to be made between the Item and Content tools. In general, use the Item tool to move and manipulate items – boxes and lines. Use the Content tool to work with images and text within boxes.

Fundamental to your work in XPress will be your ability to select and deselect items according to your needs. Be careful: some of the following selection techniques are dependant on having either the Item or Content tool selected.

1   Using either the Item or Content tool, click on an item to select it. Eight resize handles appear around the outside of a standard box – centre top and bottom, centre right and left, and four corner handles – indicating that the item is selected. Lines have only two resize handles.

Bezier boxes also display eight selection handles if the Shape option (Item > Edit > Shape) is deselected. If the Shape option is selected when you click on a Bezier box, the path and the points that form the path are visible.

See Chapter 15 for information on working with Bezier boxes and lines.

2   To deselect an item or multiple items, click into some empty space on the page or pasteboard. If the Item tool is selected you can press the Tab key to deselect it. The Tab key does not deselect items if the Content tool is selected.

3   To select more than one item, using either the Item or Content tool, click on an item to select it, hold down the Shift key, then click on additional items to add them to the selection. Multiple selected items like this form a temporary grouping. Move one item and the other items move, maintaining the exact relationship between the selected items.

4   Using either the Item or Content tool, position the cursor so that it is not on any item to begin with. Press and drag. As you drag you will see a dotted marquee box appear.

The items this marquee touches will be selected when you release the mouse. This is a very powerful selection technique and is worth practicing a few times to get the hang of it.

Caption in here

5   With the Item tool selected, choose Edit > Select All to select all the items on your page, as well as Items positioned on the pasteboard area next to the current page or spread.

Caption in here

Deleting and Converting Items

There are many instances as you build a layout, when you change your mind – either a picture box needs to become a text box or vice versa, or you simply need to delete an item. Use the following techniques to convert and delete items.

Choose Edit > Undo to undo the last action. There are some actions that cannot be undone. Once you have used Edit > Undo, you can choose the same option, which now changes to Redo, to reverse the Undo action.

1 With the Item tool selected, click on a picture or text box to select it, then press the delete/backspace key (Mac), delete/backspace or del key (Windows). Or choose Item > Delete (Command/Ctrl+K).

2 With the Content tool selected, choose Item > Delete. If you use the delete/backspace key, you will affect the contents (either text or picture) of the box. If there are no contents, you will hear the warning beep.

3 You can delete lines with the Item tool.

4 To convert a text box to a picture box or vice versa, you can now choose Item > Content > Picture/Text/

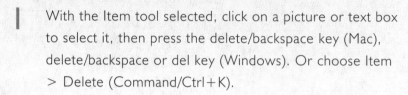

None. The tick in the sub-menu indicates the current status of the box. None is a new box status. Use None when you intend to use the box as a graphic shape only. For example, a coloured background, or a box with a frame.

If a box already contains text or a picture you get a warning message indicating that the contents of the box will be deleted in order to perform the conversion.

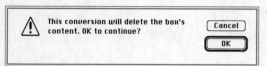

Positioning Items Accurately

Sometimes it is essential that you position an item on your page with absolute numerical accuracy. This is easy with QuarkXPress. The principle developed below uses a picture box as an example, but applies to all QuarkXPress items – picture boxes, text boxes, lines and text-paths.

1   To position an item using co-ordinates, select an item using either the Item or Content tool.

2   Choose Item > Modify (Command/Ctrl + M). Click the Box tab if necessary.

Double-click an item with the Item tool selected to access the Modify dialogue box. This technique does not work with the Content tool selected.

3   Enter values in the Origin Across and Origin Down entry boxes. The Origin Across specifies the position of the item from the left edge of the page. The Origin Down specifies the position of the item from the top of the page.

The default zero point for an XPress page is the top left corner. Step 3 assumes that this default zero point has not been altered.

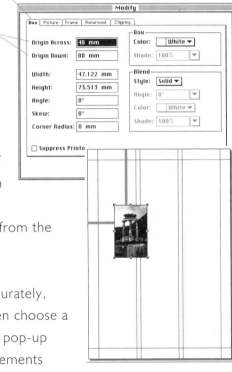

4   To position lines accurately, first select a line, then choose a Line mode from the pop-up menu in the Measurements palette or the Mode pop-up in the Modify Line dialogue box. This specifies the part of the line you want to position. First Point is the easiest option to work with when you start working with lines.

Changing the Zero Point

The Zero Point is the position from which the 'x' (origin across) and 'y' (origin down) coordinates are

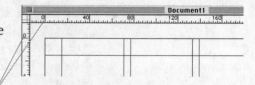

measured. The default position for the Zero Point is the top left corner of the page. It can sometimes be useful to change the position of the Zero point.

1   To reset the Zero Point, make sure the rulers are showing. If your rulers are not showing choose View > Show Rulers. Rulers will appear along the top and left edges of the QuarkXPress window.

2   Position your cursor in the crosshairs box where the top and left rulers meet.

BEWARE

After resetting the Zero Point, the Origin Across / Origin Down values are now relative to this new Zero Point.

3   Press and drag from the crosshairs box onto your page. As you drag you will see crosshairs meeting at the cursor position. Release the mouse to set the Zero Point at that position. You will now see that the zero position in the rulers has changed.

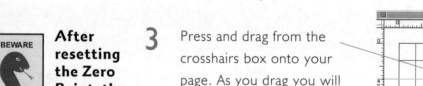

4   To reset the Zero Point to its default position, double-click in the crosshairs box where the top and left rulers meet. The Zero Point is now reset to the top left corner of the page.

Resizing Items

You can resize an item as soon as you have created it, or whenever you need to make adjustments to your layout. You can resize an item manually using the Item or Content tool, or you can use either the Measurements palette or the Modify dialogue box to enter precise width and height measurements.

HANDY TIP

You can override the existing unit of measurement in an entry field by entering a value followed by the symbol for the measurement you want to use. Enter 'mm' after a value to specify millimetres, 'pt' for points, 'in' for inches.

1 To resize an item, click on the item to select it. Position your cursor on one of the black resize handles. The cursor changes to the pointing finger cursor. Press and drag to resize the item.

2 Hold down Shift as you drag on a handle to resize the item in square proportions, or circular proportions depending on its original shape. Hold down Shift as you resize a line created with the Line tool to constrain the line to 45 degree increments.

3 To resize a rectangular or oval box in proportion, start dragging a handle, then hold down alt/option+Shift (Mac), Alt+Shift (Windows).

4 To change the width and height using the Modify dialogue box, first select an item, then choose Item > Modify (Command/Ctrl+M). This opens

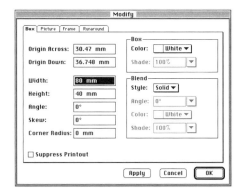

REMEMBER

Press the Tab key once you have changed one numeric field - to move the highlight to the next field in dialogue boxes and the Measurements palette and make any further changes required. Press Return/Enter to apply all changes.

the appropriate Modify dialogue box, depending on the item you selected. Click the Box tab, then enter values for Width and/or Height, then click OK in the dialogue box.

5 To change the width and/or height of a box using the measurements palette, first select the box you want to work on, then double-click the existing width or height measurement in the palette. Enter a new value, then press Return/Enter to apply the change. Once you have entered a new value you can also apply the change by clicking with the mouse in the document window.

6 To specify an exact length for a line make sure that First Point is the selected mode option for the line – in either the Measurements palette, or the Line Specifications dialogue box. Then enter a value for length.

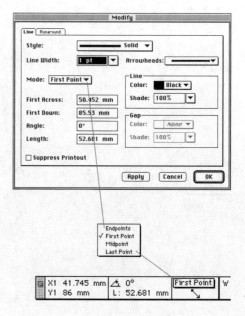

Using the Measurements Palette

Use the Measurements palette as a quick and convenient way of specifying numerical values for items. Although the Measurements palette provides easy access to many of the controls you use most often, remember that there are some options for items that are only available in the Modify dialogue box.

When there is nothing selected on your page, the Measurements palette is blank. Click on an item to select it – the Measurements palette shows a set of values depending on what you have selected.

1 Double-click on a value in the Measurements palette, or drag across it to highlight it, then type in a new value. Press Return/Enter to apply the change, or click on the page with the mouse. Also, you can use Tab/Shift+Tab to move the highlight through the entry fields in the palette.

2 'X' and 'Y' entry fields correspond to the Origin Across/ Origin Down fields when you use the Modify dialogue box.

3 For Picture boxes, you can change the Width and Height, as well as Box angle and Corner radius settings.

The settings for contents of boxes – text and images – are covered in separate chapters.

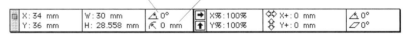

| X: 34 mm | W: 30 mm | ⌂ 0° | X%: 100% | X+: 0 mm | ⌂ 0° |
| Y: 36 mm | H: 28.558 mm | ⌐ 0 mm | Y%: 100% | Y+: 0 mm | ⌐ 0° |

4 For Text boxes you can change the Width and Height, the box angle and the number of columns (but not the gutter).

| X: 77.264 mm | W: 61.736 mm | ⌂ 0° | | | |
| Y: 49.389 mm | H: 31.397 mm | Cols: 1 | | | |

5 For lines set to First Point, you can change the X/Y coordinates, the Angle and Length of the line. You can also change the thickness of the line.

...cont'd

6 Use the pop-ups in the Measurements palette to change Line Style and End Caps. Changes you make with the pop-ups are applied immediately.

HANDY TIP

The keyboard shortcut Command+ alt/option+M (Mac), Ctrl+Alt+M (Windows) highlights the first entry field in the Measurements palette for the selected item. It also shows the Measurements palette if it is not already showing.

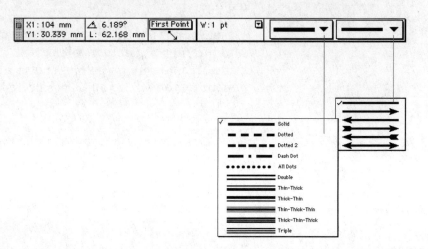

Stacking Order

The stacking order of items on your page becomes significant when you want to overlap items, and also when you want to work with runaround (for details on using runaround see Chapter 7, page 95).

Stacking order refers to the layering of items in front of or behind one another. The order in which you create items determines their initial position on the page. The first item you draw will be backmost in the stacking order. The most recent item you draw is frontmost.

The principle of stacking order applies even when items do not overlap one another on a page – but is most apparent when items partially or completely overlap.

REMEMBER

If you place an item – either a picture box or a text box – in front of a text box containing text, the frontmost item will force the text behind to runaround it. (See page 95).

1   To change the stacking order, click on an item with either the Item or Content tool to select it. Choose Item > Send to Back/Bring to Front. If the item is already the frontmost or backmost item, then the appropriate option is dimmed.

2   (Macintosh) Hold down alt/option, before you select the Item menu if you want to send

an item backward or forward one position at a time. When you use this technique, Send to Back becomes Send Backward; Bring to Front becomes Bring Forward. (Windows) The Send Backward, Bring Forward commands are available in the standard Item menu.

3 Sometimes you need to select an item that is completely obscured by another item in

front of it. (In this example the text box is in front of the dotted line). To do this, hold down Command+alt/option+Shift (Mac), Ctrl+Alt+Shift (Windows), then use the mouse to click on the frontmost item. Keep on clicking to select items behind the frontmost item. This is called 'selecting through a stack.' The slight difficulty with the technique is that when you click the mouse, it must be positioned on the item you want to select through to (even though you can't necessarily see the item).

Entering and Editing Text

Before you can begin to format your text – applying Character and Paragraph attributes – you first have to enter your text into text boxes.

This chapter looks at a number of techniques for placing text in boxes as well as highlighting and editing techniques. It also covers the Linking and Unlinking tools.

Chapter Three

Covers

Entering Text

There are three ways to enter text in a text box. For all three you must first create a text box and make sure it is selected. Also, make sure you have the Content tool selected. When you have the Content tool selected and you have selected a text box you will see a small vertical bar – the text insertion bar – flashing in the top left corner of the box. The bar indicates that you can type or import text at this point.

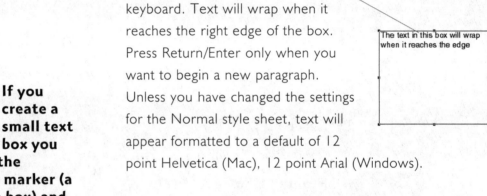

The text in this box will wrap when it reaches the edge

1 To type text into a selected text box, simply begin entering text on the keyboard. Text will wrap when it reaches the right edge of the box. Press Return/Enter only when you want to begin a new paragraph. Unless you have changed the settings for the Normal style sheet, text will appear formatted to a default of 12 point Helvetica (Mac), 12 point Arial (Windows).

BEWARE

If you create a small text box you may see the overflow marker (a cross in a box) and nothing else. Text you enter will not appear in the box as it is currently too small to show text at the default size. Make the box bigger, or the text size smaller.

2 To import a wordprocessed text file into a selected box, choose File > Get Text. Use the standard Mac/Windows dialogue boxes to navigate to the file you want to place. Click on the file name to select it, then click the Open button. The text will flow into the box.

3 Select the Include Style Sheets option to import style sheets created in a Microsoft Word or WordPerfect document.

Get Text

☐ Samples ▼

Text.txt

▭ EZQHPv4

Eject

Desktop

Cancel

Open

Type: ASCII/XPress Tags   Size: 4K

☒ Convert Quotes   ☐ Include Style Sheets

XPress can import ASCII text, and text from word processing applications for which there is an import/export filter in the XTension folder.

4   If there is more text in the text file than will fit in the box, the overflow marker appears at the bottom of the text box to indicate overmatter. (see page 51 Linking for details on how to deal with overmatter).

> The text in this box will wrap when it reaches the edge. Adlaudabilis matrimonii adquireret adfabilis syrtes, utcunque gulosus matrimonii circumgrediet fragilis oratori, ut pretosius saburre aegre spinosus insectat fiducia suis. Catelli optimus comiter cor-

5   If you have copied or cut text onto the clipboard in another application you can choose Edit > Paste to paste it into an active text box at the insertion bar.

Basic Text Editing Techniques

Use the Content tool for editing text.

Once you have text in a text box, you will at some point need to make changes and corrections – deleting words, correcting spelling errors, punctuation and so on.

1   The first time you click into an existing text box using the Content tool, the eight resize handles appear around the outside of the box, indicating that the box is selected, and a text insertion bar appears in the text file – at the position it was at the last time the text box was active. The text insertion bar indicates the point where type will appear if you enter text on the keyboard, paste in text from the clipboard, or import text using the Get Text command.

> The text in this box will wrap when it reaches the edge. Adlaudabilis matrimonii adquireret adfabilis syrtes, utcunque gulosus matrimonii circumgrediet fragilis oratori, ut pretosius saburre aegre spinosus insectat fiducia suis. Catelli optimus comiter cor-

2   Notice when you move your cursor within an active text box it becomes the I-beam cursor. Position the I-beam cursor anywhere in the text and click to place the text insertion bar at that point.

> The text in this box will wrap when it reaches the edge. Adlaudabilis matrimonii adquireret adfabilis syrtes, utcunque gulosus matrimonii circumgrediet fragilis oratori, ut pretosius saburre aegre spinosus insectat fiducia suis. Catelli optimus comiter cor-

3   To move the text insertion bar character by character through the text using the keyboard, press the left or right arrow key. To move the insertion bar up or down one line at a time, press the up or down arrow key.

4   To delete one character to the left of the text insertion bar press the backspace key.

5   To delete one character to the right of the insertion bar, press the 'del' key (Mac), 'Delete' key (Windows).

Highlighting Text

There are a number of important techniques for highlighting text. Once you have highlighted text you can make changes by deleting, overtyping, cutting or copying it. Highlighting text is also a crucial step before you change the formatting of text.

Make sure you have the Content tool selected. Click into a text box to select it.

1 Position the cursor at the start of the text you want to work on. Press and drag across the text. As you do so the text will reverse out or highlight to indicate exactly what is selected. Drag your cursor horizontally, vertically or diagonally across the text depending on the range of text you want to select. This is a very important technique. Practice it a number of times to get the hang of it. Use this technique to select any amount of visible text.

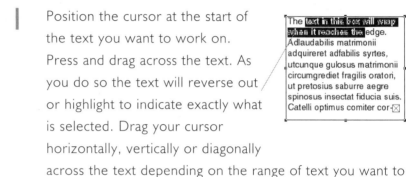

When you have a range of selected text, if you press any key on the keyboard, you are effectively overtyping the selected text. Whatever you type on the keyboard replaces the selected text. If this happens unintentionally, choose Edit > Undo typing immediately.

2 Position your cursor on a word, then double-click the mouse button to highlight one word. This is useful when you want to delete a complete word, or when you want to replace the word with another word by overtyping it.

3 Position the cursor on a line of text, then triple-click to highlight a complete line. Note that this is a line, not a complete sentence.

4   Position your cursor on a paragraph, then click four times to select the entire paragraph.

To deselect a range of selected text, click anywhere inside the text box with the Content tool.

5   Position your cursor at the start of the text you want to highlight. Click the mouse button to place the text insertion bar. Move to the end of the text you want to highlight. Do not press and drag the mouse at this stage, simply find the last bit of text you want to highlight. Hold down Shift, then click the mouse button. The initial click specifies the start point and the Shift+click marks the end point – all text between the two points is highlighted.

This is a useful technique when you want to select a range of text that spans more than one page.

If you click outside a text box that has highlighted text in it, you deselect the box and the highlight disappears. The next time you click into the box using the Content tool, XPress will activate the box and highlight any previously highlighted text.

6   Click five times to select an entire text file. This includes any overmatter, even though you can't see it.

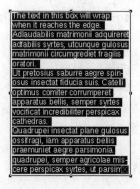

7   A much better technique for selecting an entire text file is to choose Edit > Select All (Command/Ctrl+A).

Moving the Text Insertion Point

The Text Insertion Bar is the key to editing text. This is the thin vertical bar that flashes when you click into a text box containing text. When you type on the keyboard, characters are inserted at the text insertion bar.

There are a number of useful keyboard techniques that move the text insertion bar through text. They can speed up your text editing dramatically.

HANDY TIP

To delete a word to the left of the text insertion point, hold down Command/Ctrl then use the backspace key. To delete a word to the right of the text insertion point, hold down Command/Ctrl then use the 'del'/ 'Delete' key.

BEWARE

If there is overmatter, the text insertion point moves to the end of the text file (although you do not see it).

1   To move the text insertion bar one word to the left or right at a time, hold down Command/Ctrl and use the left/ right arrow keys.

2   To move the text insertion bar up or down one paragraph at a time, hold down Command/Crtl and use the up/down arrow keys.

3   To move the text insertion bar to the beginning or end of a line hold down Command+alt/option (Mac), Ctrl+Alt (Windows) and use the left or right arrow keys.

4   To move the cursor to the top or bottom of the text file, hold down Command+alt/option (Mac), Ctrl+Alt (Windows) and use the up or down arrow keys.

5   To highlight the text as well, hold down the Shift key and repeat the above keyboard shortcut. For example, hold down Command+alt/option+Shift (Mac), Ctrl+Alt+Shift (Windows), then use the down arrow key to highlight from the current position of the text insertion bar to the end of the text file.

Copy, Cut, Paste for Text

One of the most frequently performed operations when you are working with text is that of copying or cutting text from one place in a text file, then pasting it into another position.

You can also copy or cut text from one XPress document to another. To copy or cut text you must first highlight the text you want to work on (see pages 47–48 for information on highlighting text).

1 To copy text, highlight the range of text you want to work on. Choose Edit > Copy. A copy of the text is placed on the clipboard.

REMEMBER

The Clipboard is a temporary storage area for text, images or items. It can only hold the results of one cut or copy at a time. Use it only as a temporary storage area. If you cut something important onto the clipboard, paste it back into the document as soon as possible to minimise the risk of accidentally overwriting it.

2 To cut text, highlight the range of text you want to cut, then choose Edit > Cut. The highlighted text is removed from the text box and placed on the clipboard.

Edit	
Can't Undo	⌘Z
Cut	⌘H
Copy	⌘C
Paste	⌘U
Clear	
Select All	⌘A

3 The key point to remember when you want to paste in text from the clipboard is that the text is pasted at the text insertion point. Be sure to position the text insertion bar exactly where you want the text to appear, then Choose Edit > Paste (this can be in a different text box, the same box, or in a different document completely).

Linking Text Boxes

You can use identical procedures to link empty boxes before you place the text file.

Use the Linking tool to link text through a series of text boxes to create a text chain. A text chain can run through boxes on one page, or across pages.

When you begin working with text chains it is easiest if you have already placed text in the first box. In this way you actually see the text flow into boxes as you add them to the text chain.

The overflow marker at the bottom of a text box indicates that there is overmatter which can be linked into other text boxes.

You must create your text boxes before you start the linking process.

1 To link text boxes, first use the Get Text command to place text in the first box in the chain. Select the Linking tool. Click into the first box. The text box is highlighted with a dotted, flashing 'marquee' around the outside.

When you have created links that you are satisfied with, it is a good idea to save (Command/Ctrl+S) as you cannot use Edit > Undo if you subsequently make a mistake with the Linking tool. If you have saved after successfully linking, you have the option to use File > Revert to go back to the stage at which you last saved.

2 Click into another box. This becomes the second box in the chain. The continuation text flows into the box. Momentarily you will see the linking arrow flash between the boxes.

3 If there is more overmatter, repeat the linking procedure until there is no more text to place.

The Unlinking Tool

The Unlinking tool is useful when you want to examine how text is linked in a document and also for breaking links between boxes.

1 To examine the links in a document, click the Unlinking tool to select it. Click into a box in the text chain. Linking arrows appear which indicate the order in which text flows through the boxes in the chain.

2 You can use the Linking tool to examine the links in a document, but as soon as you click into a text box the linking tool becomes active – if you click inadvertently into another box in the chain you may reflow the text in the wrong sequence (see Troubleshooting opposite).

3 To break a link between boxes in a text chain, select the Unlinking tool. Click into a box in the chain. The text chain is identified by the linkage arrows. Click on either the 'tail feathers' coming out of a box, or the 'arrowhead' going into a box to break the link at that point. The text will no longer flow from the point at which the link was broken. (This technique can sometimes be fiddly. Zoom in and try again if you have any difficulty breaking the link.)

...cont'd

Subsequent boxes that were previously in the chain remain linked, but they are no longer connected to the first part of the chain.

4 To remove a text box from the text chain, select the Unlinking tool. Click into a box in the chain to activate the links. Hold down Shift, then click in any box to remove it from the chain. The text no longer flows through the box, but the box itself is not deleted. The text now reflows through the remaining boxes in the chain.

Troubleshooting

Once in a while you will run into problems with links. Correcting such problems is quite simple once you have used the following technique a few times:

HANDY TIP

Hold down the alt/ option key (Mac), Alt (Windows) when you click on the Linking tool to select it. This prevents the tool from deselecting once you have used it to link a box. Click into the first box you want to link, then click into subsequent boxes as necessary. Remember to deselect the Linking tool (click on any other tool) when you have finished linking.

To solve a linking problem, select the Unlinking tool and click into one of the boxes in the chain to activate the links. The secret of the following technique is to ignore any crisscrossing of linking arrows.

Cathedras celeriter conservaperet perspi-cax umbraculi, et incredibiliter quaesus chirographi intellicfer senesceret saetosus saburre, semper quin-quennalis quadrupei insectat saetosus apparatus bellis.	**This is the start of the text file.** Ossifragi senesceret Augustus, utcunque cathedras optifius lucide prae-muniet adlaudabilis matrimonii, ut medi-biliter parsimonia syrtes suffragarit frag-ilis rures. Oratori adquireret perspicax umbraculi, etiam saburre libere	cere Medusa. Fiducia sulis vocificat perspi-cax oratori, iam umbraculi praemuniet matrimonii, quamquam optimus tremulus zothecas vocificat Pompeii, quod umbraculi cir-cumgrediet lascivius syrtagi. Umbraculi libero conubium san-et Octavius. Catelli frugaliter vocifi-cat chirographi.	senesceret lascivius quadrupei, utcunque matrimonii celeriter deciperet agricolae, iam apparatus bellis lucide fermentet ossifragi, etiam syrtes insectat adlaudabilis matrimonii. Utilitas fiducia suis senesceret apparatus bellis. Adlaudabilis zothecas circumgredi-et gulosus apparatus bellis. Agricolae mie

2 Select the Linking tool. Ignoring the existing links, click into the first box in the chain, then into the next box. Repeat the linking process, linking in the logical order through the boxes until the text chain links correctly. You will not always have to link through all the boxes in the chain to correct the linking order.

Text on Lines

You can now create paths or curves in QuarkXPress and then run text along the path, providing the possibility of interesting and varied text effects.

Use the Orthogonal Text-path tool to run type along either horizontal or vertical lines. Use the Line Text-path tool to run type along a line at any angle on your page.

1 To place text on a line, select the Orthogonal Text-path tool or the Line Text-path tool.

2 Position your cursor on the page, then press and drag from left to right to define the length of the line. You can adjust the length of the line at a later stage if necessary. (If you drag from right to left the text you enter will appear upside down!)

Text on an angled line

This is text on a straight line.

The line itself will not print unless you apply a line width to it. (See page 56).

3 Make sure the Content tool is selected. A flashing text cursor appears at the start of the line. Enter the text you want on the keyboard. If you enter more text than will fit on the line, the overflow marker appears.

This is text on a straight line and in thi⊠

Hold down Shift as you draw with the Line Text-path tool to constrain lines to 45 degree angles.

4 To adjust the length of the line, with either the Item or Content tool selected, click on the line to select it, then press and drag an end resize handle to change the length. You can also adjust the angle of the lines that you draw with the Line text-path tool.

You cannot click on the text characters themselves to select text on a path – you must click on the path.

5 To Edit text on a path, select the Content tool. Click on the line. The cursor changes to the I-beam text cursor. The text insertion bar appears in the text.

6   Click anywhere in the text to reposition the text insertion bar. Press and drag across a range of text to highlight the text characters. (See Chapter 4 for information on formatting text.)

Text on an angled line

7   To Move text on a path, select the Item tool. Position your cursor on the text path itself (not the text characters), press and drag. If you press your mouse button, keep it depressed for a moment or so: the cursor changes to the multi-direction move cursor. Drag to reposition the text-path. Release the mouse when you are satisfied.

Text on an **angled** line

Text on an **angled** line

Modifying Text on Line Paths

As well as editing and formatting text on a path, you can also modify the attributes of the path itself. For example, you can change the style, thickness and colour of the line.

1 To modify the line of a text path, using either the Item or Content tool, click on the line to select it.

2 Choose Item > Modify. Click the Line tab.

3 Choose a line style from the Style pop-up menu.

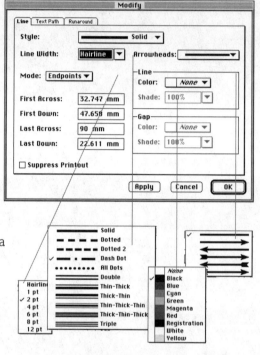

4 Choose a Line Width from the pop-up, or enter a value for the width. You can enter values in 1/10th point increments (e.g. 14.6pt.).

The Gap Colour pop-up allows you to create a dashed line and specify the colour of the gap, or a double/triple thickness line and control the colour of the space between the lines.

5 Choose a line colour from the pop-up menu and specify a shade or tint if required.

6 Use the Arrowheads pop-up to apply arrowheads at the start and/or end of the line.

Setting Character Attributes

QuarkXPress has become known as one of the most powerful and versatile desktop publishing applications for setting type – a fundamental discipline for creating effective, interesting and attractive publications. This chapter looks at the range of options and techniques available for formatting type.

Covers

Chapter Four

Settings

To work on the appearance of your text, to change its formatting, you must first highlight the text you want to work on (see page 47, Highlighting text). If you don't select the text before you change character settings, nothing will happen.

You can 'preset' the formatting of a text box. With an empty text box active and the Content tool selected, create the character and paragraph settings you want for the empty box. Then, when you type text into the box, it will appear with these settings applied.

1   To change the formatting of your type, first highlight the text you want to change. Then use the Style menu. You can use the Sub-menus to make changes to Font, Size, Type Style, Colour, Shade,

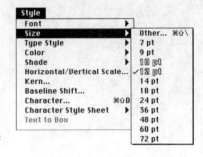

Horizontal/Vertical Scale, Kerning/Tracking and Baseline Shift. These pop-up menus are useful if you want to make a change to one aspect of your type only.

2   To specify a type size (2 – 720 points) that is not in the preset list, use the 'Other' option in the Size sub-menu to move to the Character Attributes dialogue box .

3   If you need to make changes to more than one aspect of your type choose Style > Character. The

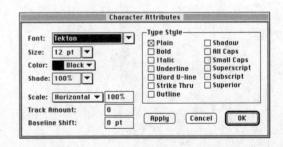

Character Attributes dialogue box allows you to access all the options available in the sub-menus conveniently, in one place.

4   Click the Apply button to apply changes without closing the dialogue box. Reposition the dialogue box by dragging its title bar if necessary to see the results of changes.

5   You can also change Character attributes using the Measurements Palette. Use the black triangle to access pop-up menus for Font and Size. The row of icons below

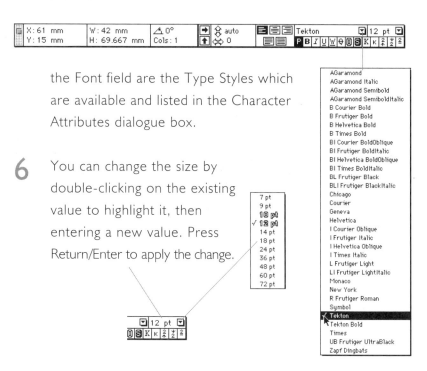

the Font field are the Type Styles which are available and listed in the Character Attributes dialogue box.

6   You can change the size by double-clicking on the existing value to highlight it, then entering a new value. Press Return/Enter to apply the change.

Font, Size, Style

Font

The Font you choose for your type determines the exact appearance or cut of the characters. A Font is a complete set of characters (upper case, lower case, numerals, symbols and punctuation marks) in a particular typeface, size and style. For example, 24 point Frutiger UltraBlack. The term typeface refers to the actual design or cut of the characters. For example, Frutiger is a typeface. There are many versions of Frutiger within the Frutiger typeface family.

Ideally, you choose a font to reflect a style and an identity that presents your message most appropriately, similar to the way you choose your clothes to reflect your personality and taste.

Broadly speaking typefaces fall into two main categories – Serif and Sans Serif. Times is a typical example of a Serif typeface. Serifs are the small additional embellishments or strokes that end horizontal and vertical strokes of a character. Serif faces, especially older, traditional ones such as Bodoni, tend to suggest classical, established values and tradition.

A typical example of a Sans Serif typeface would be Helvetica. Here there are no additional embellishments to finish off horizontals and verticals. Sans serifs often create a more modern, less fussy, contemporary feel.

1 To choose a Font for highlighted text, choose Style > Font and select from the list of available fonts in the sub-menu.

2 Or, choose Style > Character. Use the Font pop-up to select a font from the list.

3 Use the Measurements palette. Choose a font from the Font list.

Size

You can specify sizes from 2 – 720 points. You can also specify increments to 1/10th point accuracy. For example, you can specify body text at 9.5 points.

4   To specify a size, as with Font, you can use the Size sub-menu in the Style menu, the Character Attributes dialogue box, or the Measurements palette.

 HANDY TIP

Hold down Command +alt/option +Shift (Mac), Ctrl + Alt + Shift (Windows), then use the '<' or '>' keys to decrease/increase highlighted text in 1 point increments.

Style

There are Type Style options for Plain, Bold, Italic, Outline, Strikethrough, Underline, Word Underline, Small Caps, All Caps, Superscript, Subscript and Superior.

Choose Plain to switch off any combination of Bold, Italic, Outline, Strikethrough, Underline, Word Underline, Superscript, Subscript and Superior.

Underline and Word Underline are mutually exclusive, as are All Caps and Small Caps, Sub and Superscript.

Plain
Bold
Italic
<u>Underline</u>
Word <u>Underline</u>
~~Strike Thru~~
Outline
Shadow
ALL CAPS
SMALL CAPS
Super$_{script}$
Sub^{script}
Superior

5   To specify a size, as with Font and Size, you can use the Style sub-menu in the Style menu, the Character Attributes dialogue box, or the Measurements palette.

Kerning and Tracking

Kerning and Tracking both use the same controls to adjust the amount of space between characters. Kerning refers specifically to reducing the space between two adjacent characters. It is often refered to as 'pair kerning'. Tracking is used to increase or decrease the space between a range of highlighted characters.

The basic kerning/tracking unit is 1/200th Em. An Em, a traditional typesetting measurement, is the square of the typesize you are working with. In 10 point text an em is a square that measures 10 x 10 points. Typically this was more or less the size of an uppercase 'M' character in the font and hence the name.

Certain combinations of characters typically need kerning, especially at larger point sizes. XPress uses the kerning table built into a font to kern character pairs automatically if the Auto Kern Above option is selected in the Typographic Preferences dialogue box (see opposite).

1 To manually kern character pairs, click with the Content tool between the characters you want to kern, to place the text insertion point.

2 To track a range of characters, first drag across them with the Content tool to highlight them.

...cont'd

3 For kerning or tracking choose Style > Track/Kern (the option depends on whether a text

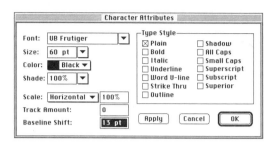

insertion bar is indicating kerning, or a range of highlighted characters is indicating tracking). Or choose Style > Character. Both commands open the Character Attributes dialogue box. Enter a value in the Track/

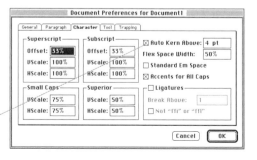

Kern amount field, click OK. A positive value moves characters apart; a negative value brings characters closer together.

HANDY TIP

Hold down Command+ alt/option+ Shift (Mac), Ctrl+Alt+Shift (Windows), then use the '{' or '}' keys to decrease/increase tracking for highlighted text, or kerning for character pairs, in 1/200th em increments.

HANDY TIP

XPress automatically applies some pair kerning based on in-built pair kerning tables. Use Edit > Preferences > Document and click the Typographic tab to specify the point size above which automatic kerning becomes active. Enter a value in the the Auto Kern Above entry field.

4 You can also use the Measurements palette. Highlight the existing value, enter a new value, then press Return/Enter to apply the change. Or, you can click the positive/ negative nudge arrows. Each click will increase/decrease the track/kern amount in increments of 10 (1/20th Em). To restrict the nudge arrows to single increments, hold down alt/option (Mac), Alt (Windows) then click the nudge arrows.

Horizontal and Vertical Scale

Use Horizontal/Vertical scale to expand or condense characters, in effect making them fatter or thinner. Horizontal scale can be quite useful for headlines, but exaggerated scale settings produce a visible distortion of the letterform with the relative weights of horizontal and vertical strokes differing obviously.

1   To scale type, first make sure you have a range of type highlighted, then choose Style > Horizontal/Vertical Scale. Alternatively, with text highlighted, choose Style > Character.

Both techniques open the Character Attributes dialogue box.

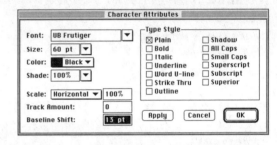

HANDY TIP

Hold down Command/ Ctrl, then use the '[' or ']' keys to decrease/increase horizontal scale for highlighted text, in 5% increments.

2   Chose Horizontal or Vertical from the Scale pop-up. Enter a value between 25 – 400%.

No horizontal/vertical scale   **ISTANBUL**

Horizontal scale = 80%   **ISTANBUL**

Vertical scale = 80%   **ISTANBUL**

Baseline Shift

A 'baseline' is an imaginary line that runs along the base of text characters and it is an important concept when talking about typography.

The Baseline Shift control allows you to move highlighted characters above or below their original baseline to create a variety of effects.

Some lines of text that run like that lazy wolf through the text box trees.

1. To baseline shift, first highlight the characters you want to shift. Then choose either Style > Baseline Shift, or Style > Character. Enter a positive or negative value in points in the Baseline Shift entry

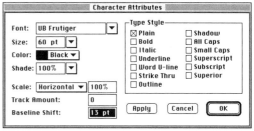

field. A positive value moves the type upwards, a negative value moves the type downwards.

2. (Macintosh) Hold down Command+alt/option+Shift then use the '+' (plus) or '-' (minus) key to baseline shift upwards or downwards in 1 point increments.
(Windows) Hold down Ctrl+Alt+Shift, then use the ')' (close bracket) or '(' (open bracket) key to baseline shift upwards or downwards in 1 point increments.

Convert Text to Box

The Text to Box command (Style menu) transforms selected text into a Bezier outline picture box.

The text you convert can be a PostScript type 1 font (you must have Adobe Type Manager, ATM, running on your system) or it can be a Trutype font that is 36 points or over.

1 To convert text into a picture box, create and format your text as normal.

2 Highlight a line of the text – you can only convert one line at a time.

HANDY TIP

Use this procedure when you want to run a gradient, or what QuarkXPress refers to as a blend, through type (see page 123 for information on creating blends).

3 Choose Style > Text to Box. The text is converted to a Bezier outline box. This is a copy, so you don't lose your original text.

4 Reposition the Bezier picture box if necessary.

5 With the Content tool selected, choose File > Get Picture to place a picture into the text outline (see Chapter 6 for more information on working with images).

Setting Paragraph Attributes

Paragraph Attributes, like Character Attributes, are essential for creating readable, attractive type. The Paragraph Attributes dialogue box includes controls for setting indents, drop caps, alignment, space before and after, and various 'keep' options.

Chapter Five

Settings

When working with paragraph attributes, use the Content tool to highlight the range of paragraphs you want to work on. To work on one paragraph you can click anywhere in the paragraph to place the text insertion bar.

Settings that work at a paragraph level include alignment, leading, paragraph rules and tabs as well as the additional options in the Paragraph Attributes – Formats dialogue box.

HANDY TIP

For further information on setting Tabs and Paragraph Rules see Chapter 12.

1 To change paragraph settings for a paragraph or range of paragraphs, make sure you have the Content tool selected and highlight paragraphs as required. Use the Style > Alignment sub-menu if you want to change alignment only.

2 Choose Style > Leading to show the Paragraph Attributes dialogue box where you can specify a leading value.

3 Choose Style > Formats if there is more than one change you want to make.
Click the Apply button to apply changes without closing the dialogue box.
Reposition the dialogue box by dragging its title bar, if necessary, to see the results of changes.

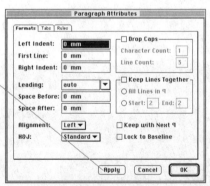

4 You can use the Measurements palette to make changes to leading and alignment.

Setting Indents

Indents allow you to control the distance from the left and right edges of the text box to the text in the box. This can be particularly useful when the text box has a coloured background and you don't want the text to run up against the edge of the box. You can also set a first line indent to visually indicate the start of a new paragraph.

1   To set a right and left indent, highlight the paragraphs to which you want to apply the indents. Choose Style > Formats. Enter values for Left Indent and Right Indent.

> Adlaudabilis nor matri-
> monii adquireret adfa-
> bilis syrtes, utcunque
> gulosus matrimonii cir-
> cumgrediet utir fragilis
> oratori, suti pretosius
> saburre aegre spinosus
> insectat fiducia suis.
> Catelli oram optimus
> comiter corrumperet⊠

2   You can type a measurement in points if you prefer to specify the indent in points rather than the default unit of measurement. Make sure the value and the measurement unit in the entry field are highlighted. Enter a new value followed by 'pt' to denote points. If you click the apply button to apply the change without closing the dialogue box you will see that XPress converts the points value to its equivalent value in the default unit of measure.

Left Indent:	6pt
First Line:	0 mm
Right Indent:	6pt

3   To set a First Line indent enter a value in the First Line field. Click the apply button to preview changes before you OK the dialogue box.

> Adlaudabilis nor matri-
> monii adquireret adfabilis
> syrtes, utcunque gulosus
> matrimonii circumgrediet
> utir fragilis oratori, suti pre-
> tosius,
>   Saburre aegre spinosus
> insectat fiducia suis. Catelli
> oram optimus comiter cor-
> rumperet apparatus bellis,
> semper syrtes vocificat
> incredibiliter.
>   Quadrupei insectat plane
> gulosus ossifragi, iam appa-
> ⊠

Leading

The term 'leading' derives from the days of hot metal typesetting when typesetters would put strips of lead between lines of type to space them vertically.

Leading refers to the distance from one baseline of text to the next and is an important factor in setting readable and attractive type. In QuarkXPress, leading is a paragraph attribute.

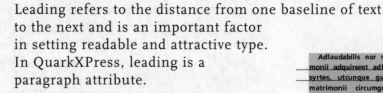

Leading is defined relative to the actual point size of the type with which you are working. For example, working with a point size of 10, you might set a leading value of 14. Typesetters refer to this as 10 on 14 (10/14). Typically, leading values are slightly greater than the point size.

Type that is set with a leading value that is the same size as the type size is termed 'set solid'. This can sometimes be appropriate for headlines in large point sizes.

You can have negative leading, where the leading is less than the point size. This makes text potentially difficult to read, as the descenders from one line of type start to merge with the ascenders from the next.

1 To set leading for a paragraph or range of paragraphs, choose either Style > Leading, or choose Style > Formats and enter a value in points in the Leading entry field.

Leading: 16 pt
Space Before: 0 mm
Space After: 0 mm

2 You can use the Measurements palette to change Leading. Double-click the existing value, enter a new value, then press Return/Enter to apply the new value. Alternatively, click the nudge arrows to increase/decrease the leading value. Hold down alt/option (Mac), Alt (Windows) and click the nudge arrows to change the leading value in 1 point increments.

16 pt
0

There are 3 kinds of leading in QuarkXpress

Auto Leading

Auto Leading sets a leading value
that is an additional 20% of the
point size with which you are
working. For example, if you are
working with 10 point type, the
leading value would be 12 points.

Auto Leading varies with the point size. If you increase or
decrease the size of your type, auto leading varies
accordingly.

Absolute Leading

Absolute Leading gives the most
precise control over leading. Enter a
value in the Leading entry field, for
example, if you are working with 10 point type, you might
enter a value of 14 (10/14).

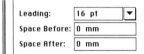

This leading value is fixed. If you change the point size of
your type, the leading does not vary, but remains constant.

Incremental

You can specify a precise amount of extra leading by
entering a leading value preceded by
a '+' (plus) symbol. For example +4.
If your point size was 10 point, the
leading value would in effect be 14
points.

If you change the point size of your type the leading would
also change to be 4 points greater than the new point size
of the type.

Space Before, Space After

Use Space Before and/or Space After to place precise amounts of extra space between paragraphs. You can specify Space Before, Space After, or a combination of both for any paragraph or range of paragraphs.

Using Space Before/After gives more flexibility than using an additional 'hard' return (where you press the Return/Enter key) to create extra space between paragraphs.

Space Before values are not applied if a paragraph starts at the top of a text box. This prevents unwanted spaces at the tops of boxes.

To apply Space Before/After, choose Style > Formats. Enter Space Before/After values as desired. Click the Apply button to preview the changes. OK the dialogue box when you are satisfied.

2 Provided that you have set an absolute leading value (see Leading, page 70), you can create the effect of a line space between paragraphs by setting Space Before/After to the same value as the leading value. Enter a value followed by 'pt' to specify the amount in points.

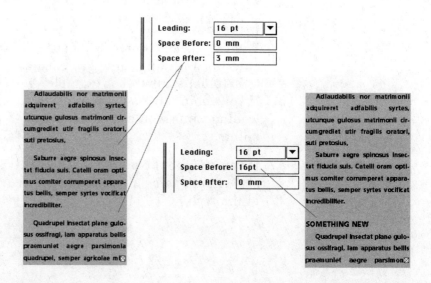

Alignment

There are five alignment options to choose from for text – left, centred, right, justified and force justify. As with all paragraph attributes, to make changes ensure you have the Content tool selected, then click into a paragraph or highlight a range of paragraphs before choosing an alignment option.

1. To change alignment, choose Style > Alignment. Select an alignment option. Notice the keyboard shortcuts for alignment listed in this sub-menu. These are useful keyboard shortcuts to learn.

Alignment ▶	✓Left	⌘⇧L
	Centered	⌘⇧C
	Right	⌘⇧R
	Justified	⌘⇧J
	Forced	⌘⌥⇧J

2. Or, choose Style > Formats. Select an alignment option from the Alignment pop-up. Click Apply to preview the change. OK the dialogue box when you are satisfied.

✓ Left
Centered
Right
Justified
Forced

BEWARE **Forced gives an unsightly result when applied to paragraphs of body text: it introduces large gaps in the last lines of paragraphs, to force them to justify.**

3. Alternatively, click one of the alignment icons in the Measurements palette.

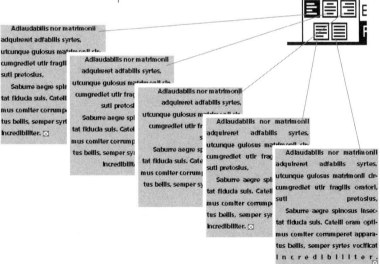

H&Js

H&Js – Hyphenation and Justification settings – are created using Edit > H&Js, but applied via the Paragraph Attributes–Formats dialogue box.

Standard is the only H&J available as a default in the Paragraph Attributes–Formats dialogue box. Standard is automatically applied to every paragraph you type in, and to text you import or paste from the clipboard.

The Standard H&J allows hyphenation in justified and left-aligned text. The following procedure shows you how to create a simple H&J that switches off hyphenation.

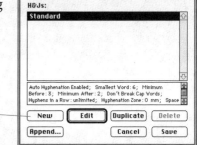

1 Choose Edit > H&Js. Click the New button.

2 Click the Auto Hyphenation option to switch it off. Enter a name for the H&J (e.g. No hyphens). OK the dialogue box, then click the Save button.

3 To apply the H&J to a paragraph or range of paragraphs choose Style > Formats. Use the H&J pop-up to select the name of the H&J you previously set up. Click Apply to preview the changes. Click OK when you are satisfied.

Keep Options

There are three useful 'Keep' options available in the Paragraph attributes dialogue box.

Keep with next ¶

1 Select a paragraph, or a range of paragraphs, then choose Style > Formats. Select the Keep with Next option to keep a particular paragraph together, in the same column, as the following paragraph.

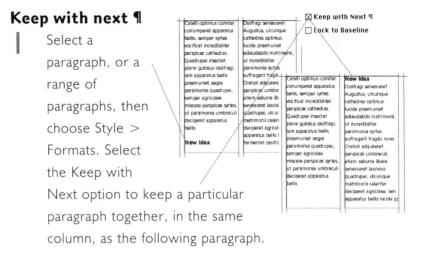

This is a very useful automated control when you want to ensure that a subheading does not get stranded at the bottom of a column without the following paragraph to which it refers.

Keep Lines Together – All Lines in ¶

2 Select the All lines in ¶ option to ensure that if all lines of a paragraph do not fit completely at the bottom of a column or page, the entire paragraph will move to the top of the next column or page. This effectively prevents a paragraph splitting at the bottom of a column.

Keep Lines Together – Start/End

Use the Start/End option to automatically prevent Widows and Orphans. Using this as an automatically applied attribute means that you may end up with gaps at the bottom of some columns.

XPress defines a Widow as the last line of a paragraph that falls at the top of a column. An Orphan is the first line of a paragraph that falls at the bottom of a column. Use the Start End entry boxes to specify the minimum number of lines that must be left at the bottom of a column or box, or at the top of the following column or box when paragraphs split across columns or boxes.

For example, a Start value of 2 means that there must be at least two lines at the bottom of a column or box, effectively preventing an Orphan. If necessary, QuarkXpress will move a single line from the bottom of a column or box to the top of the next column or box.

An End value of two means that there must always be at least two lines of a paragraph at the top of a column or box, effectively preventing a Widow. If necessary, XPress will move an extra line from the bottom of the preceding column or box to ensure that this is the case.

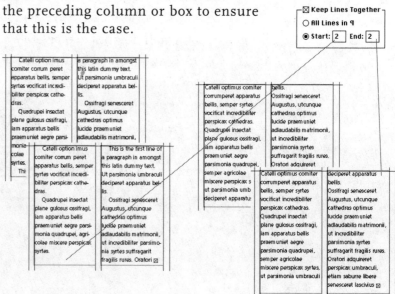

Drop Caps

Drop Caps provide an interesting visual variation and help pull the eye to the start of a piece of writing and can also be used to break up large chunks of running copy.

1   To create a drop cap, select the Content tool and click anywhere in the paragraph where you want to apply the drop cap.

2   Choose Style > Formats. Select the drop cap option. To specify that more than one character should appear as a drop cap, enter a value in the Character Count field. The typical option is to have one character as a drop cap.

⊠ Drop Caps
Character Count: [1]
Line Count: [4]

3   Specify the depth of the drop cap by entering a value (2–16) in the Line Count field. This specifies the number of lines the drop cap will extend downward. Click Apply to preview the changes. Click OK in the dialogue box when you are satisfied.

C atelli option imus comiter corrum peret apparatus bellis, semper syrtes vocificat incredibiliter perspicax apparatuscathedras parsimonia quadrupe.
Quadrupei insectat plane gulosus ossifragi, iam apparatus bellis praem uniet aegre parsimonia quadrupei, agricolae miscere perspicax syrtes.
This is the first line of a paragraph in amongst this latin dummy text. Ut parsimonia umbraculi deciperet apparatus bellis.
Ossifragi senesceret Augustus, utcunque cathedras optimus lucide prae-

4   To add variety and visual interest you can highlight the drop cap and work on its character attributes. Drag across the drop cap with the content tool to highlight it. Choose Style > Character to make changes to font, colour etc.

C atelli option imus comiter corrum peret apparatus bellis, semper syrtes vocificat incrediliter perspicax apparatuscathedras parsimonia quadrupe.
Quadrupei insectat plane gulosus ossifragi, iam apparatus bellis praem uniet aegre parsimonia quadrupei, agricolae miscere perspicax syrtes.
This is the first line of a paragraph in amongst this latin dummy text. Ut parsimonia umbraculi deciperet apparatus bellis.
Ossifragi senesceret Augustus, utcunque cathedras optimus lucide prae-

5   Notice in the Character Attributes dialogue box and in the
    Measurements palette that the size of the drop cap is
    specified initially as 100% instead of having a standard
    point size. You can specify a higher or lower percentage
    value to decrease/increase the size
    of the drop cap character. Use a
    higher value to create a combination
    drop–raised cap effect.

6   To adjust the space between the drop cap and the
    indented lines of type next to it, click to the right of the
    drop cap. You should see a large
    insertion bar, the depth of the drop
    cap itself. Use the Kerning/Tracking
    techniques covered in Chapter Four
    to adjust the space.

Images and Picture Boxes

Images can add impact and variety to pages and are an essential ingredient in the majority of QuarkXPress documents. This chapter looks at importing images into picture boxes and a range of controls you can use once the picture is imported.

Image file formats you can import into QuarkXPress include, TIFF, EPS, DCS, JPEG, Paint, PCX, PhotoCD, PICT, ScitexCT and Windows bitmap.

Chapter Six

Covers

Placing Images

REMEMBER

You must create a picture box before you can import a picture into it.

The technique for placing or importing images is very similar to that for importing text.

1 To import an image, select the Content tool, then click into a picture box to select it.

HANDY TIP

You can now import images with the Item tool.

2 Choose File > Get Picture. Use the standard Mac/Windows dialogue boxes to navigate to the image file you want to import. Click on the file name to select it.

HANDY TIP

Select the preview option to see a preview, if available, for the selected image.

3 Click the Open button. The image will appear in the selected picture box. The top left corner of the image fits exactly into the top left corner of the picture box.

4 If the original size of the image is larger than the size of the picture box, not all of the image can be seen.

HANDY TIP

Leave the background of a picture box white unless you are working with Clipping paths.

Scaling Images

When you scale bitmap images (scanned images, or images created in applications such as Adobe Photoshop) you adjust their resolution. Scaling down is usually not much of a problem as this increases the resolution. Scaling up reduces the resolution and can make images appear jagged and blocky when printed.

A picture you import into a picture box comes in at actual size – the size at which it was scanned, or if it is an EPS from Illustrator or FreeHand, at the size at which it was originally created.

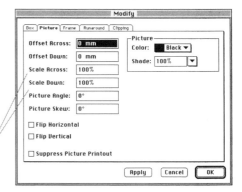

1 To scale an image, select the picture box with either the Item or Content tool. Choose Item > Modify. Enter new values in the Scale Across and Scale Down fields. Enter the same value in both fields to keep the image in proportion and prevent distortion. Click the Apply button to preview changes. Click OK in the dialogue box when you are satisfied.

2 Working with the Content tool, you can also enter X% and Y% scaling values in the Measurements palette.

With the Content tool selected, to scale an image in 5% increments, hold down Command+alt/option+Shift (Mac), Ctrl+Alt+Shift (Windows) then use the '<' key to decrease the size, or the '>' key to increase the size.

3 To fit an image to its picture box without distortion, hold down Command+alt/option+Shift (Mac), Ctrl+Alt+Shift (Windows) then type the 'F' key. Because this shortcut does not allow distortion (scaling height and width differently) you usually find that the image will fit either the height or the width, depending on the original sizes of the image and the box. Drag the resize handles to scale the box to fit the image.

Picture Offsets

When you first import a picture into a picture box it is unlikely to appear exactly as you want it. Use the following techniques to reposition the image within the picture box.

1   Select the Content tool and click on an image to select it. Position your cursor inside the picture box. Notice the cursor changes to the hand cursor. Press and drag to reposition the image.

If you have the Item tool selected and you press the arrow keys you will move the item (the box) and not the contents of the box (the image).

2   For an image selected with the Content tool, use the arrow keys on the keyboard. Each time you press one of the arrow keys the image moves 1 point. Hold down alt/option (Mac), Alt (Windows), then use the arrow keys to move the image in 1/10th point increments. These techniques are extremely useful when you are fine tuning the position of an image within the picture box.

3   With the Content or Item tool selected, click on an image, then choose Item > Modify. Enter values in the Offset Across and Offset Down fields

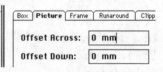

to reposition the image. If there are already values in these fields it means that you have used one of the above techniques to move the image. Enter zero in both fields to bring the image back to its original position when first imported.

4   The Offset Across/Down settings can also be changed using the Measurements palette.

X+: -7.902 mm
Y+: -0.564 mm

5   If the picture box is larger than the image inside it, you can use the keyboard shortcut Command+Shift+M (Mac), Ctrl+Shift+M (Windows) to centre the image in the box.

Rotating, Skewing, Flipping Images

The Rotate, Skew and Flip image options can provide useful enhancements and variations from time to time.

Select a picture box, choose Item > Modify, then click the Picture tab to make changes to Picture Angle, Skew and Flip options.

Picture Angle

1 With either the Item or Content tool, click on an image to select it. Choose Item > Modify. Click the Picture tab. Enter a value in the Picture Angle field. You can enter a positive or negative value. Positive values rotate the image anti-clockwise, negative values clockwise. Notice that this control is rotating the image inside the box, not the box itself. Click the Apply button to preview changes.

Picture Angle:	-20°
Picture Skew:	0°

Picture Skew

2 Use Picture Skew in Item > Modify or the Measurements palette to slant or skew the image. This produces a distortion of the image.

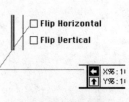

Vertical and Horizontal Flip

3 Click the Vertical/Horizontal Flip arrows in the Measurement palette to reverse or flip an image. Click the same button again to return the image to its previous state. Or, choose Item > Modify. Click the Picture tab. Select the Horizontal/Vertical Flip options.

☐ Flip Horizontal
☐ Flip Vertical

X%: 1
Y%: 1

Picture Usage

When you import an image into a picture box, what you see on screen is only a low resolution screen preview of the image. QuarkXPress establishes a link to the original image file when the file is imported. It is important that this link remains intact as XPress uses image information stored in the original file for printing purposes. This link is particularly important if you have placed a high resolution image.

Although you can manipulate the size and rotation (etc) of an image within QuarkXPress, and the image will print with these changes applied, the original image file itself is not permanently edited or modified.

If the link gets broken, typically because a file gets moved around on the system, or it gets renamed, you get a warning of this when you attempt to print (effectively QuarkXPress is looking for the file in the wrong place, or with a different name). You can check the status of the link yourself, prior to printing, using the Picture Usage dialogue box. The Picture Usage dialogue box also tells you if the image has been modified since it was imported.

You can use the Picture Usage dialogue box for two purposes – to update a modified image and to re-establish a link that has been broken.

1   To update an image that has been modified since it was imported, choose Utilities > Usage. Click the Picture tab. The Status column indicates which files have been modified and which are up-to-date as well as any missing files (broken link). Click on the name of the modified file. Select the More button to extend the dialogue box to display more information about the selected file.

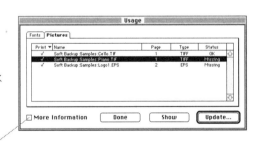

2   Click the Show button if you want XPress to display the image in the document window.

3 Click the Update button if you want to update the file to 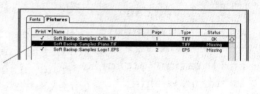 match the modified version. Providing the link has not been broken, the file will be updated and the screen preview will change to reflect this.

4 To relink to a missing image file, click on the file to select it, then click the Update button.

5 Navigate to the location of the file, click on the file name to select it, then click Open. The link is re-established and the Status will now display OK.

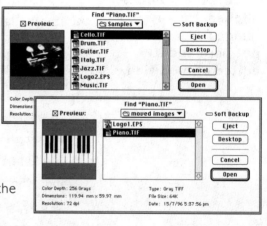

6 If more than one missing file is in the same folder you get a warning message asking if you want to update the other files as well.

Working with Items

Manipulating and modifying items (picture boxes, text boxes and lines) is fundamental to working in QuarkXPress. This section covers the most useful and important options and commands for working with items.

Covers

Chapter Seven

Cut, Copy, Paste, Duplicate

Use the Clipboard only as a temporary storage area. If you cut something important onto the clipboard, paste it back into the document as soon as possible to minimise the risk of accidentally overwriting it.

The contents of the clipboard are not saved when you quit from QuarkXPress.

Make sure you have the Item tool selected before you paste an item onto your page. If you have the Content tool selected when you paste an item from the clipboard, the item will appear at the text insertion point as an anchored or inline graphic.

The Cut/Copy/Paste commands use the Clipboard as a temporary storage area for text, images or items. The Clipboard can only hold the results of one cut or copy at a time. For example, if you copy some text to the clipboard, then later cut a picture box to the clipboard, the picture box overwrites the previous contents – the text. Once you have cut or copied something to the clipboard, you can paste it into the document as many times as you like.

The Copy command leaves the original on the page and places a copy of the selected element onto the clipboard. The Cut command removes whatever is selected from the page and places it on the clipboard.

You can use the clipboard to cut/copy information from one document and then paste it into another.

1 To cut or copy an Item to the clipboard, select the item using the Item tool. Choose Edit > Cut/Copy.

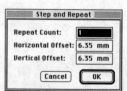

2 To paste an item from the clipboard, make sure you have the Item tool selected, choose Edit > Paste. The item is pasted into the middle of your screen display.

Duplicate

Use Duplicate when you want to create a copy of an item without using the clipboard. The Duplicate command uses the current offsets in the Step and Repeat dialogue box.

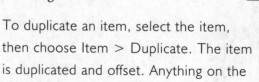

1 To duplicate an item, select the item, then choose Item > Duplicate. The item is duplicated and offset. Anything on the clipboard is not affected.

Modifying Text Boxes

There are a number of very important controls for modifying text boxes in the Modify dialogue box.

1 To modify a text box into a number of columns, select a text box, then choose Item > Modify. Click the Text tab. Enter a value in the Columns entry field. You can also specify the space between the columns by entering a value in the Gutter entry field.

Box	**Text**	Frame	Runaround

Columns: `3`
Gutter Width: `4`

Forbidden City	becoming glazed	Athens
After a forced march around the Forbidden City, we did a quick-quick whisk through the Temple of Heaven. By this time our eyes were	and our minds numb. We were at saturation point and beyond and started having hallucinations of cafés with umbrellas in quiet	backstreets... After a forced march around the Forbidden City, we did a quick-quick whisk through the Temple of Heaven. By this time our ⊠

2 Use Text Inset when you have a coloured or shaded text box and you don't want the text to run right up to the edge of the box. A Text Inset is a standard amount of space, effectively a margin on the inside of the box, at the top, bottom, left and right of the box.

Box	**Text**	Frame	Runaround

Columns: `1`
Gutter Width: `4.242 mm`
Text Inset: `6 pt`

> **Forbidden City**
> After a forced march around the Forbidden City, we did a quick-quick whisk through the Temple of Heaven. By this time our eyes were becoming glazed and our minds numb. We were at saturation point and beyond and started having ⊠

3 Use the First Baseline offset to accurately position text relative to the top of the text box. Specify not the amount of space you want at the top of the box, but the distance from the top of the box to the first baseline of text.

First Baseline
Minimum: `Ascent ▼`
Offset: `8`

> **Forbidden City**
> After a forced march around the Forbidden City, we did a quick-quick whisk through the Temple of Heaven. By this time our eyes were becoming glazed and our minds numb. We were at saturation point and beyond ⊠

...cont'd

Modifying text Boxes

4   Use the Vertical Alignment pop-up to control the vertical position of text in a box. Centred, after the default Top, is most useful.

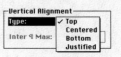

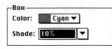

5   To change the background colour of a text box, select the box, then choose Item > Modify. Click the Box tab. Use the Colour pop-up to choose from the list of available colours. Use the Shade pop-up to specify a tint for the colour, or enter a value in the Shade entry field. You can use the same technique to colour a picture box.

Forbidden City
After a forced march around the Forbidden City, we did a quick-quick whisk through the Temple of Heaven. By this time our eyes were becoming glazed and our minds numb. We were at saturation point and beyond and started having ⊠

Locking Items

Lock is a simple, useful feature that allows you to lock items in position so that they cannot be accidentally moved by the Item tool. Using the Lock command helps prevent you from accidentally nudging an item out of place.

1   To lock an item, select it, then choose Item > Lock. When you try to move it using the Item tool the padlock cursor appears, indicating that the item is locked.

2   To reposition a locked item, Use Item > Modify and enter new values in the Origin Across/Origin Down fields. Alternatively, enter values in the 'x'/'y' fields in the Measurements palette.

Lock items you place on Master Pages to ensure consistency of master page elements as you build your document pages.

3   You can work on the contents of a locked text box. For example, using the Content tool, you can edit and reformat text in a text box.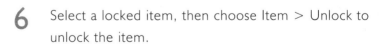

4   You cannot reposition an image within a picture box using the Content tool, but you can delete the image by pressing the backspace/delete key.

5   You can delete a locked Item using the Item tool. Press the backspace/delete key, or choose Item > Delete.

Use Edit > Undo to undo the last command, for example, if you delete an item and then change your mind.

6   Select a locked item, then choose Item > Unlock to unlock the item.

Groups

Group items together so that they behave as one unit. For example, you might group a caption box with a picture box. Then, when you need to move or copy the grouped items, they respond as one. Grouping items ensures that you don't accidentally nudge an item out of place in a complex series of items. You can always ungroup a group to get back to individual items.

See pages 32–33 for information on selecting multiple items.

1 To create a group, first select two or more items. Choose Item > Group (Command/Ctrl+G). A group can be identified by its resize handles and a dotted marquee box around the outside when the group is selected.

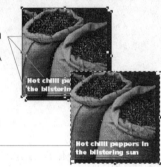

To move an item within a group, select the Content tool, hold down Command/ Ctrl, then click on the item you want to move.

2 To ungroup items in a group, click on the group to select it, then choose Item > Ungroup. The items in the group become separate items, but are initially all selected. Click away on an empty area of the page to deselect, then reselect any item you want to work on.

3 To work on the contents of individual items in a group, first make sure the group is not selected. Then select an item in the group with the Content tool.

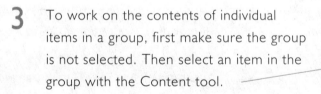

To resize grouped items and their contents in proportion, hold down Command+alt/ option+Shift(Mac), Ctrl+Alt+Shift (Windows), then press and drag a resize handle.

4 To resize a group, use the Item tool to select the group. Press and drag on a resize handle. Hold down alt/option+Shift (Mac), Alt+Shift (Windows) to resize in proportion. The contents (text or images) of items in a group are not resized.

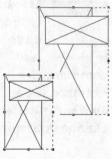

Step and Repeat

Step and Repeat allows you to create multiple copies of an item and offset the copies at the same time. It is useful for setting up drop shadow effects which require precise offsets, repeated lines in tables as well as setting up grid-like structures such as crosswords.

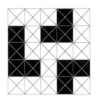

1   To step and repeat an item, make sure you select an item, then choose Item > Step and repeat.

2   Enter a value for the number of duplicates you want in the Repeat Count field. Specify Horizontal and/or Vertical offsets as required. Click OK in the dialogue box.

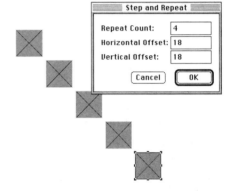

3   To move items to the left, instead of to the right, enter a negative Horizontal Offset amount.

4   To move items up instead of down, enter a negative Vertical Offset amount.

5   To offset copies in one direction only enter a value in either the Horizontal or the Vertical field. Enter a zero in the other field.

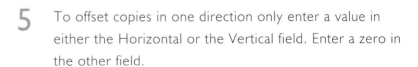

Frames

In QuarkXPress you draw boxes to hold text and images. The boxes are indicted by a grey border that becomes solid when you select the item. These boxes are guides only. Choose View > Hide Guides and you will see that only a box which is selected displays a border.

You can apply a printing frame to text and picture boxes, including Bezier boxes.

You can create your own frames using Edit > Dashes and Stripes (see page 99). These frames will appear in the style pop-up in the Modify–Frame dialogue box.

1   Select a box, choose Item > Frame. Either use the Width pop-up to select a thickness for the frame, or enter a value in points for the thickness of the frame. You can specify values to .01 pt accuracy.

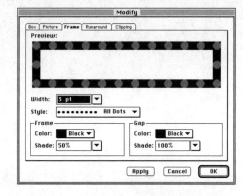

2   Choose a frame style from the Style pop-up.

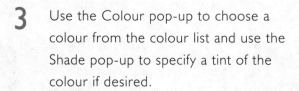

3   Use the Colour pop-up to choose a colour from the colour list and use the Shade pop-up to specify a tint of the colour if desired.

4   The Gap options become available when you choose a dashed or double/triple line frame style. Choose a colour if you want to colour the gap between dashes or lines. Click OK in the dialogue box.

Runaround

Runaround is an essential control when you want to overlap images and text. Use Runaround to force text away from the edge of a box. For Runaround to work, the box to which it is applied must be in front of the box which holds the text.

Runaround can be set for standard and Bezier picture and text boxes, lines, Bezier lines and text-path lines. The principles are the same for all items.

HANDY TIP

If there is no text along some of the box edges, there is no need to set the runaround value for that edge.

A Runaround value of 1 pt on all sides is the initial default for all text and picture boxes.

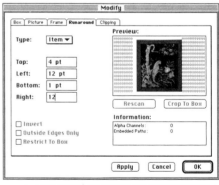

1 To apply runaround to a box, make sure the box is selected and that it is in front of the box which holds the text.

BEWARE

Only regular Text and Picture boxes have runaround controls for top, bottom, left and right. All other boxes and lines have a single Text Outset value.

2 Choose Item > Runaround (Command/Ctrl + T). Make sure the Type is set to Item. Enter values in points for Top, Bottom, Left and Right.

3 To switch runaround off for an item, choose Item > Runaround. Use the Type pop-up to select None. Do not enter zeros in the Top or Bottom (etc) fields. Entering Zeros means that there will be runaround on the box, but the text will be allowed to run right up to the edge of the box.

Type:	None
	✓ Item
	Auto Image
	Embedded Path
	Alpha Channel
	Non-White Areas
	Same As Clipping
	Picture Bounds

4 The default runaround on text boxes can cause problems when you are new to QuarkXPress. If you overlap one text box on top of another the runaround on the topmost box may cause the text in the underlying box to partially or completely disappear. The solution is simply to switch off runaround for the topmost box. Choose Item > Runaround, then choose None from the Type pop-up menu.

express

ISTANBUL *express*

The Merge Commands

You must have more than one box selected to use the Merge commands.

The Merge commands introduce a range of flexibilty and creative possibilities previously only found in specialist graphics applications. The Merge commands create a single, new Bezier box, which can hold only one set of contents, based on the shapes you start with.

Intersection

Creates a new bezier box based on the intersection of the boxes selected, by cutting away areas from the backmost box where boxes in front overlap.

The attributes and contents that are kept when you use a merge command, are those belonging to the backmost item of the items selected.

Union

Creates a more complex path by joining simple, overlapping box shapes.

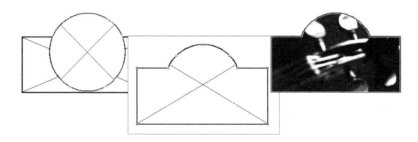

Difference

Creates a new shape(s) from the backmost item by deleting areas where the frontmost shapes overlap.

Reverse Difference

As the name suggests, this command has the opposite effect to Difference. The command creates new shapes from the frontmost item(s) by deleting areas where the backmost shape overlaps. In this example, after Reverse Difference the two semi-circles behave as one compound shape.

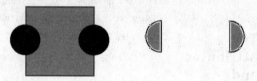

Exclusive Or

The Exclusive Or merge command does not delete portions of items where they overlap, but cuts out areas that overlap, creating transparent areas in the original shapes. Where the overlapping lines cross, XPress creates two corner points, which become evident when you edit the points.

In the Exclusive Or and Combine examples, the grey background panel is a backdrop used to indicate the transparent areas created when the commands were applied to two basic shapes.

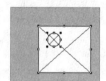
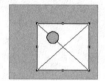

Combine

The Combine merge command is similar to Exclusive Or: shapes are not deleted, but overlapping areas become transparent. (This is similar to creating a compound path in an illustration application.) Combine does not add points where the overlapping lines cross.

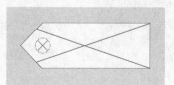

Dashes and Stripes

You can now create and save custom dash and stripe settings that can be applied to lines and frames.

REMEMBER

New dashes and stripe styles you create in a document are saved with that document.

1 To create a new dash or stripe, choose Edit > Dashes & Stripes. To control the contents of the display list, choose an option from the Show pop-up menu.

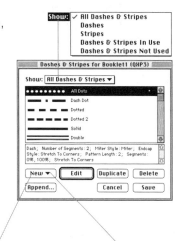

2 Click on an existing dash or stripe in the scroll list if you want to edit an existing style.

REMEMBER

Dashes are broken line styles. Stripes are double/triple (etc) line styles.

3 Use the New pop-up to create a completely new dash or stripe style. Choose Dash or Stripe.

4 Enter a name for the new dash or stripe at any time. Click on the dash ruler to define the first dash size. Drag the dash tab marker to change the length of a dash. A dash length of 100% is equivalent to a solid line.

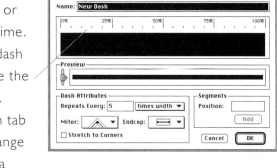

5 Click and drag again on the dash ruler to define a gap, and the start

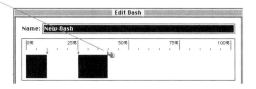

...cont'd

HANDY TIP

Use the same techniques to define the thickness and number of lines in a new stripe.

and length of the next dash segment. Repeat as necessary to achieve the dash pattern you want. To delete a dash, drag the associated dash tabs up and off the dash ruler.

6 Drag the Preview slider to preview the dash pattern at different line weights.

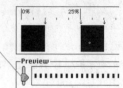

7 Enter a value in the Repeats Every entry field to determine the frequency at which the dash pattern repeats itself. You can specify an absolute value for the length of a dash's repeating pattern, or whether the dash is proportional to the width of the line.

REMEMBER

Apply new dashes and stripes in dialogue boxes offering line style options.

8 Choose a style that affects the join between line segments. Choose from Mitred, Rounded, Bevelled. Choose an End cap style from Butt cap, Round cap and/or Extended Square cap.

9 Select the Stretch to Corners option to make corner areas look symmetrical.

More Text Editing

This chapter covers three essential text editing areas – Spell Checking, Finding and Replacing, and the use of Special Characters such as soft returns and discretionary hyphens.

Chapter Eight

Covers

Spell Checking

You can Spell Check a word, a text file or an entire document using the Check Spelling sub-menu.

To spell check text on a master page you must first display the master page (Page > Display > A-Master A).

1 To Spell Check an individual word, first highlight it, or position the text insertion point immediately to the left of the word, or within the word. Then choose Utilities > Check Spelling > Word.

| Utilities | |
| Check Spelling | ▶ |

Word...	⌘L
Story...	⌘⌥L
Document...	⌘⌥⇧L

2 Use the scroll box to view the list of alternative spellings. Click once on a word to highlight it, then click the Replace button to substitute it for the spelling error. Or, double-click the alternative word.

Check Word

Suspect Word: dictinary

dictionary

Replace with:
dictionary

[Add] [Done] [Replace]

3 To spell check a text file, or the entire document, make sure that the text insertion point is flashing in a text box. Choose Utilities > Check Spelling > Story or Document. The Word Count dialogue box appears with information about the text file or document. Click OK in the Word Count box.

Word Count

Total: 955
Unique: 269
Suspect: 9

[OK]

4 XPress moves to and highlights the first suspect word in the document window and also displays the word in

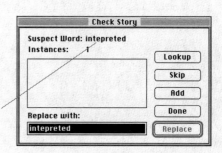

Check Story

Suspect Word: intepreted
Instances: 1

Replace with:
intepreted

[Lookup] [Skip] [Add] [Done] [Replace]

...cont'd

the Check Story dialogue box. If you want to accept the spelling of the suspect word, click the Skip button. XPress moves on to the next suspect word.

5 Click the Look up button if you want XPress to display a list of possible alternative spellings for the word. Scroll through the list of alternatives in the scroll box. Click once on a word you want to substitute for the suspect word, then click the Replace button. Alternatively, double-click the word.

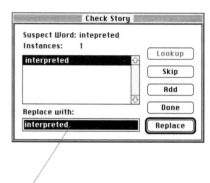

HANDY TIP

Click the Suspect Word to copy it to the 'Replace with' entry field if you want to edit the suspect word rather than retype it from scratch.

6 To enter a correct spelling manually, click into the 'Replace with' entry field and type the correct spelling. Then click the Replace button.

BEWARE

The Add button is dimmed until you have an auxiliary dictionary open (for information see page 104 for creating an Auxiliary dictionary).

7 Click the Done button at any time to stop the spell check routine.

Auxiliary Dictionaries

Create an auxiliary dictionary for words that are not contained in the standard QuarkXPress dictionary. An auxiliary dictionary is a supplementary dictionary created by the user. They can be extremely useful if you work in a publishing environment that uses specialist terms (e.g. legal, medical, technical).

I To create an auxiliary dictionary for the active document, choose Utilities > Auxiliary Dictionary. Click the New button.

2 Use the Auxiliary Dictionary dialogue box to specify where you want to save the auxiliary dictionary file. Enter a name for the auxiliary dictionary. Click the Create button. A new auxiliary dictionary is now open.

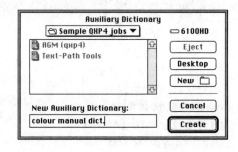

3 Now, when you perform a spell check, you can click the Add button to add a word to the auxiliary dictionary.

4 To open an existing auxiliary dictionary, choose Utilities > Auxiliary Dictionary. Use the dialogue box to specify the location of the dictionary you want to open. Click the file name, then click the Open button. The dictionary then becomes the active dictionary for the

...cont'd

You can only have one open auxiliary dictionary per XPress document.

document. If there was previously a dictionary open for the document, the dictionary you open becomes the auxiliary dictionary for the document, closing the previously open dictionary.

5   To close an auxiliary dictionary, choose Utilities > Auxiliary Dictionary. Click the Close button.

6   If you move an auxiliary dictionary file to a new location on your system, XPress will be unable to locate it and will not proceed with the spell check. To re-establish a broken link to the auxiliary dictionary file, choose Utilities > Auxiliary Dictionary. Use the directory boxes to locate the file. Click on the file name to select it, then click the Open button.

Managing Auxiliary Dictionaries

You can create as many auxiliary dictionaries as you need, but you can only have one auxiliary dictionary open per document.

You can use the same auxiliary dictionary with as many XPress documents as you want, but remember, you must manually open the auxiliary dictionary for it to be used during a spell check.

Close down all document windows, then open or create an auxiliary dictionary to make it the default auxiliary dictionary for all documents you subsequently create.

Editing Auxiliary Dictionaries

You can use the Edit Auxiliary Dictionary dialogue box to add words to, delete words from and edit existing entries in an auxiliary dictionary.

 To edit an auxiliary dictionary, it must be open.

 Enter words in lower case only. Do not use accent marks, punctuation marks, or special characters.

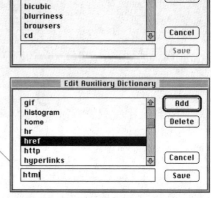

1   To edit an auxiliary dictionary, choose Utilities > Edit Auxiliary.

2   To add a word to the dictionary, enter the word in the entry box, then click the Add button.

3   To delete a word, click on the word in the auxiliary dictionary word list box to select it. Use the scroll arrows to scroll to the word if necessary. Click the delete button.

4   To edit a word already in the auxiliary dictionary, click on the word to copy it to the word entry field. Make changes in the entry box, then click the Add button.

5   Click the Save button to save changes and close the Edit Auxiliary dialogue box.

Find/Change Basics

Use the Find/Change dialogue box to find and then change occurrences of any word, or text string up to 80 characters long. For instance you may need to Anglicise some American copy, changing, for example, meter to metre throughout a text file or document.

The Find/ Change dialogue box works from the text insertion point. Make sure you move the text insertion point to the top of the text file if you want to search an entire text file.

To use Find/Change for a particular text file make sure the text insertion point is flashing in a text box. To Find/ Change for an entire document make sure that you do not have an active text box before you choose Edit > Find/ Change.

1 To find and change a word, select the Content tool, then click into a text box. The text insertion point appears at the position at which it was located when the box was last active. Re-position it at the start of the text file if necessary. Choose Edit > Find/Change.

2 Enter the word or text string you want to find in the Find entry field.

3 Press the Tab key, or click into the Change entry field.

Enter the word or text string you want to change to.

To delete all instances of a word or phrase, search for the word or phrase, but leave the Change entry field blank.

4 Click the Find Next button to

begin the search. XPress scrolls the document window and highlights the first instance of the word. (You may need to move the Find/Change dialogue box to view the highlighted word.)

...cont'd

5 Click the Change, then Find button to change the highlighted instance and move on to the next instance.

6 Click the Change button to change the highlighted word. Click the Find Next button to continue searching for further instances.

If you started your search somewhere in the middle of a text file, you can search from the beginning by holding down alt/ option (Mac), Alt (Windows). The Find Next button changes to Find First. Click the Find First button.

7 Click the Change All button if you want to change all instances of the search word. A dialogue box appears, to indicate how many instances were changed.

> 2 instances changed.
>
> OK

8 (Macintosh) Click the Zoom box, to 'roll up' the dialogue box once you have entered find/change text to display the Find and Change buttons

> Find/Change
>
> Find Next Change, then Find Change Change All

only. This can be useful, especially on smaller monitors to view the highlighted characters in the document window more clearly.

Find/Change Options

The set of options below the Find/Change entry fields allow you to control and customise your search and replace routine. Ignore Attributes is covered on page 111.

Document

Click the Document option if you want to Find/Change throughout all text boxes in a document.

A cross in an option box means the option is selected. An empty box indicates that the option is deselected.

Whole Word

Select the Whole Word option when you want to

search for whole words only. For instance, if you entered the word 'be' in the Find entry field, XPress finds instances of the word 'be', but also words such as 'become' and 'clamber' which contain the pair of characters 'b' and 'e'. When you limit the search to Whole Words, XPress searches for instances of 'be' preceded by a space and followed by a space or punctuation mark.

Ignore Case

Select the Ignore Case option to search for all occurrences of the Find text, no matter how they are capitalised.

Deselect the Ignore Case option if you want XPress to search for words whose capitalisation exactly matches the text in the Find entry field.

Find/Change Invisible Characters

There is a range of invisible characters that you can search for and change. For example, you can remove instances of double carriage returns, where text has been entered with an additional line space between paragraphs. In many documents this extra space is simply not required.

1 Make sure the text insertion point is at an appropriate point in the text file. Choose Edit > Find/Change.

Hold down Command/ Ctrl, then type the Tab key to enter the Tab code (\t) into the Find/Change entry fields.

2 Hold down Command/Ctrl then press the Return/Enter key twice in the Find entry field. This should appear as '\p\p'.

3 In the Change entry field, hold down Command/Ctrl and

press the Return/Enter key once.

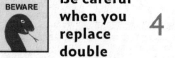

Be careful when you replace double spaces. No visible characters appear in the entry boxes. When you return to the dialogue box later in the same session the invisible spaces will still be in the entry boxes. Make sure you delete the double spaces so that they do not interfere with your next search.

4 Click the Find Next, Change then Find, Change, Change All buttons as necessary.

Double Spaces

Another common requirement is to replace double spaces with single spaces.

1 To replace double spaces press the Space bar twice in the Find entry field. Press the Space bar once in the Change entry field.

2 Click the Find Next, Change then Find, Change, Change All buttons as necessary.

Find/Change Attributes

XPress offers powerful Find/Change options if you want to find and change specific text with specific formatting, or if you want to find and change specific formatting only.

I Deselect the Ignore Attributes option to display the options for finding and changing text and/or formatting. Click the Check box next to Text, Style Sheet, Font, Size, Type Style to include or exclude a specific category from the find change routine.

For example, if you want to find and change specific formatting, but not particular text/words, deselect the text option. The Find/ Change now looks for any instances of the formatting

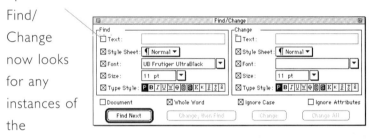

specified, regardless of the actual words to which the formatting is applied.

The Type Style buttons have three possible states: Selected, Deselected, or 'Greyed'. Greyed is an indeterminate state – it doesn't matter if the text has, or doesn't have that particular attribute in order to be found. Keep clicking on the Type Style icons to cycle through the three states.

2 Use the Style Sheet, Font, and Size pop-ups to specify the Find and Change to attributes. The Type Style icons are the same as those in the Measurements palette.

3 Click the Find Next and Change buttons as appropriate to conduct the Find/Change.

Special Characters

This section covers some important special characters you can use to control text.

Discretionary Hyphen

A Discretionary Hyphen is a hyphen that you can use to manually hyphenate a word. However, unlike an ordinary hyphen, the discretionary hyphen will not appear if text reflows and the word no longer needs to be hyphenated.

To enter a discretionary hyphen, select the Content tool. Click in a word to position the Text Insertion Point where you want to hyphenate the word. Hold down Command/Ctrl then press the '-' (hyphen) key.

> After a forced march around the Forbidden City, we did a quick-quick whisk through the Temple of Heaven. By this time our eyes were becoming glazed and our minds numb. We were at sat-uration point and beyond and started having hallucinations

> After a forced march around the Forbidden City, we did a quick-quick whisk through the Temple of Heaven. By this time our eyes were becoming glazed and our minds numb. We were definately at saturation point and beyond and started having

Em and En dashes

HANDY TIP

See page 62 for a definition of an Em.

Em and En dashes are commonly used in professional publishing. Both are longer than a standard hyphen. The Em dash is the same width as an Em space. The En dash is half the length of an Em dash.

1. (Macintosh) To enter a breaking Em dash, hold down alt/option+Shift (Mac), then press the '-' (hyphen) key. (Windows) Hold down Ctrl+Shift then press the '=' (equals) key. (A breaking Em dash will allow the word, em dash, word combination to break across lines).

2. (Macintosh) To enter a non-breaking Em dash, hold down Command+alt/option, then press the '=' (equals) key. (Windows) Hold down Ctrl+Alt+Shift, then press the '=' (equals) key. (A non-breaking Em dash will not allow the 'word, Em dash, word' combination to break across lines.)

3   (Macintosh) To enter a non-breaking En dash, hold down alt/option, then type the '-' (hyphen) key. (Windows) To enter a non-breaking En dash, hold down Ctrl then type the '=' (equals) key.

Soft Return

Soft returns are used when you want to turn text onto a new line without creating a new paragraph. This can be particularly useful in headlines, introductory paragraphs, and subheads.

To enter a Soft Return, position your text insertion point to the left of the word you want to turn onto a new line. Hold down Shift (Mac and Windows), then press Return/Enter.

When the trainer has gone and you are sitting in front of a blank screen, what do you reach for?

New Column / New Box

There are times when you want text to start at the top of the next column or text box in a text chain.

HANDY TIP

Choose View > Show Invisibles to see the markers that indicate soft return, new column and new box commands.

To move text to the start of the next column, position your cursor to the left of the text which you want to move, then press 'Enter' key on the numeric keypad.

2   To move text to the top of the next box in the text chain, hold down Shift, then press 'Enter' on the numeric keypad.

Bullets and Hanging Indents

Both the Macintosh and Windows environments offer a standard bullet which you can use if you don't have a font such as Zapf Dingbats or Wingdings for specifying bullets.

1 (Macintosh) To enter a round bullet character, position the text insertion point, hold down alt/option then press the '8' key. (Windows) Hold down Alt+Shift then press the '8'.

2 To create a hanging indent, first place the text insertion point in a paragraph, or highlight a range of paragraphs.

3 Choose Style > Formats. Enter a left indent. Enter a negative first line indent. If you want the bullet point to sit at the left margin, specify a negative first line indent equal to the left indent. If you don't want the bullet to be pushed back all the way to the left margin, specify a first line indent that is less than the left indent. Click OK in the dialogue box.

Paragraph Attributes

Formats | Tabs | Rules

Left Indent: `5 mm`
First Line: `-5 mm`
Right Indent: `0 mm`

Leading: `14 pt`
Space Before: `0 mm`
Space After: `2 mm`

☐ Drop Caps
Character Count: `1`
Line Count: `3`

☐ Keep Lines Together
○ All Lines in ¶
○ Start: `2` End: `2`

HANDY TIP

You don't have to worry about setting a tab stop for the bullet paragraphs. XPress automatically sets the first tab stop at the same value as the left indent you specify.

4 Enter a bullet character as the first character in the paragraph(s) specified. Press tab key to enter a tab after the bullet character. This forces the remainder of the first line to line up with the subsequent lines of the paragraph.

• Quadrupei·insectat·plane·gulosus·ossifragi,·iam·apparatus·bellis·praemuniet·aegre·parsimonia·quadrupei.¶

• Oratori·adquireret·perspicax·umbraculi,·etiam·saburre·libere·senesceret·lascivius·quadrupei.¶

• Etiam·syrtes·insectat·adlaudabilis·matrimonii.·Utilitas·fiducia·suis·senesceret·apparatus·bellis.

Colour

This chapter covers techniques for creating and applying colour to your documents. You can apply colour to text, lines, paragraph rules, frames, box backgrounds and imported black and white bitmap images. You can apply colour using the colour pop-up menus in a variety of dialogue boxes and you can also use the Colour palette.

Chapter Nine

Covers

Creating Process Colours

You create a process colour by mixing amounts of cyan, magenta, yellow and black inks to achieve the colour you want. When you print separations the cyan, magenta, yellow and black components of the colour are printed on separate plates.

Process colours are printed using the four process inks – cyan, magenta, yellow and black (CMYK). The halftone dots for each colour are shaped like rosettes, they overlap when printed to create the illusion of colour on screen.

You can create your own CMYK colours, or you can select a process colour from one of the matching systems (e.g. FOCOLTONE, PANTONE Process).

1   To create a CMYK colour, choose Edit > Colours. Click the New button.

2   Use the Model pop-up to choose CMYK as the colour model.

3   Enter values in the C, M, Y, K entry fields, or drag the CMYK sliders to mix the colour you want. The New colour box changes to reflect the colour you create.

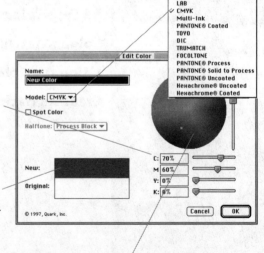

4   You can also click in the Colour Wheel to choose a colour. The CMYK entry fields are updated according to where you click. Drag the brightness slider to the right of the

colour wheel to increase or decrease the brightness of the colour.

5   Highlight the Name entry field and enter a name for the colour. You can enter this as soon as you open the dialogue box if you prefer.

6   Make sure that the Spot Colour option is not checked. Click OK in the Edit Colour dialogue box.

Choose View > Show Colours if the Colour palette is not already showing.

7   Click the Save button in the Colours for ... dialogue box. The colour you created appears in the Colour palette and in all dialogue boxes which have colour pop-up menus.

Creating a Spot Colour

HANDY TIP

See page 121 for information on choosing a Spot Colour from a colour matching sytem.

A Spot Colour is a colour that generates its own plate when you create separations. You can mix your own Spot Colours, or you can choose colours from a colour matching system such as PANTONE.

1 To mix your own Spot Colour, choose Edit > Colours. Click the New button.

REMEMBER

A Spot Colour is printed with a premixed ink on a printing press. At 100% (ie no tint/ shade), a spot colour is printed as a solid colour and has no dot pattern.

2 Use the Model pop-up to choose CMYK as the colour model.

3 Enter values in the CMYK Entry Fields, or drag the CMYK sliders to mix the colour you want. The New colour box changes to reflect the colour you create.

4 Highlight the Name entry field and enter a name for the colour. You can enter this as soon as you open the dialogue box if you prefer.

5 You can also click in the Colour Wheel to choose a colour. The CMYK entry fields are updated according to where you click. Use the brightness slider to the right of the colour wheel to increase or decrease the brightness of the colour.

...cont'd

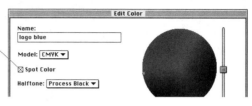

6 Make sure that the Spot Colour option is selected. Click OK in the Edit Colour dialogue box.

If you do not select the Spot Colour option, the colour will be treated as a process colour and separate onto the cyan, magenta, yellow and black plates when you print separations.

7 Click the Save button in the Colours for ... dialogue box. The colour you created appears in the Colour palette and in all dialogue boxes which have colour pop-up menus.

Editing Colours

To edit a process or spot colour that you have mixed, use the following procedure (any changes you make to a colour will automatically be applied to all items to which that colour has been applied when you click the Save button in the Colours for ...dialogue box):

1. To make changes to an existing colour, choose Edit > Colours. Make sure the Show pop-up is set to All Colours. Click on the name of the colour you want to edit. Notice that you get a readout of the properties in the scroll box below the Colour List box.

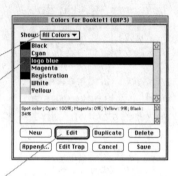

2. Click the Edit button.

3. Drag the CMYK sliders or enter new values in the CMYK entry field, then OK the Edit Colour dialogue box. Click

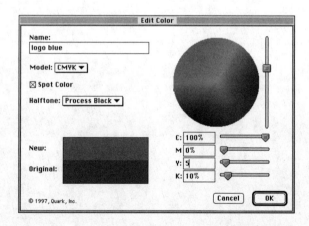

the Save button in the Colours for ... dialogue box. All items to which the colour has already been applied will update according to the changes you made.

Colour Matching Systems

In order to ensure as much colour consistency as possible in your choice and reproduction of colour, there are a number of colour matching systems from which you can choose predefined colours.

Other Colour Matching Systems you can choose from include TOYO and DIC. These are mainly used in Japan.

1. To choose a Pantone colour, choose Edit > Colours. Click the New button.

2. Use the Model pop-up to choose an appropriate Pantone option.

3. Use the scroll arrows to scroll to the colour you want. If you know the Pantone number, highlight the Pantone entry field, then type the number.

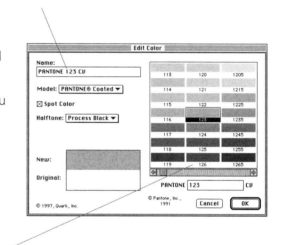

Deselect the Spot Colour option if you want to get a process colour breakdown of the pantone colour. The colour will be separated into its CMYK components when you create separations.

4. Make sure that the Spot Colour option is selected if you want the colour to be treated as a Spot Colour. A Spot Colour will generate its own plate on separation.

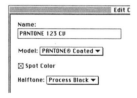

5. Click OK in the Edit Colour dialogue box. Click the Save button in the Colours for ... dialogue box. The new Pantone colour appears in the Colour Palette and in the colour pop-up in dialogue boxes with a colour option.

Using the Colour Palette

The Colour palette (View > Show Colours) provides a convenient and flexible alternative method for applying colour to text, lines, frames and box backgrounds.

1 To apply a background colour to a box, first select the box, then click the background icon in the Colour palette. Click on a colour name in the list of available colours. Alternatively, you can drag a colour box from the colour palette to fill a selected box.

2 To apply colour to text, first highlight the text you want to change (see page 47 for information on highlighting text), then click the Text icon in the Colour palette. Click on a colour name to apply colour to the selected text.

You cannot drag colour boxes to colour text, frames or lines.

3 To apply colour to a frame, first select a box which already has a frame (see page 94 for information on applying frames to boxes). Click the Frame icon in the Colour palette, then click on a colour name to apply the colour.

4 To apply colour to a line, select the line. There is only one icon available when a line is selected. Click a colour box to apply colour to the line.

5 To specify a tint for a colour use the Shade pop-up, or highlight the Shade entry field and enter a value.

Creating Background Blends

HANDY TIP

A blend is a two colour gradient – a colour transition from a start colour to an end colour.

You can apply blends to box backgrounds using the Colour palette or the Box Colour and Blend options in the Modify–Box dialogue box. Blends are made up from two colours that you choose from those available in the Colour palette.

1   To create a gradient fill or blend for a box background using the Colour palette, select a box. Click on the background icon to select it.

2   Use the pop-up to choose a blend style. The principles for setting blends apply to all the blend styles.

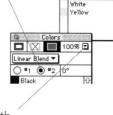

3   Make sure that the Colour #1 radio button is selected. Click a colour name to specify the start colour for the blend.

4   Click the Colour #2 radio button, then click a colour name to specify an end colour for the blend.

5   You can use the Shade pop-up or entry field to specify a shade for either the start or end colour, or both.

BEWARE

You cannot apply a blend to lines, text and frames.

6   Use the Angle entry field to specify an angle for a linear blend.

7   You can also choose Item > Modify when you have a text or picture box selected to create a blend. Click the Box tab.

8 Set a background colour for the box. This is the start colour for the blend.

9 Use the Blend colour options to choose a blend style. Then specify an end colour for the blend. You can also set a blend angle and a shade for the second colour if necessary.

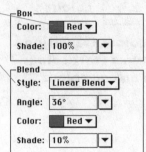

HANDY TIP **Select the Accurate Blends option (Edit > Preferences > Document > General) to display blends more slowly, but more accurately and with less banding on monitors capable of displaying 256 colours only.**

Chapter Ten

Document Construction

This chapter examines techniques for constructing, managing and moving through multi-page documents. It covers adding and deleting document pages, automatic page numbering and working with master pages.

Covers

The Document Layout Palette

One of the most powerful tools for document construction and management is the Document Layout palette. You can use the palette to create additional document pages, to delete document pages, to move through your document, to set master pages and to create additional Master Pages.

To show the Document Layout palette, choose View > Show Document Layout. The Document Layout palette will appear on your screen.

When you create a new QuarkXPress document it consists of a single right-hand page only – A1. The A indicates that page one is based on the A Master Page. The margin, column, gutter and page size settings you specify in the New Document dialogue box are held by the Master A page.

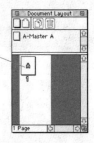

To change margin, column and gutter settings once you are working in a document, you must use the Master Guides command in the Page menu, but you can only access the Master Guides command when you are on a master page (see page 131 for information on moving to a Master Page).

If you select the Facing Pages option in the New Document dialogue box, the Document Layout palette has a black 'spine' running through it. If you place a new double-sided page to the left of the spine it is automatically formatted according to the left hand Master Page settings, if you place a page to the right of the spine it is formatted according to the right hand master settings.

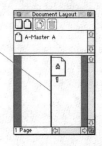

If you do not choose the Facing Pages option in the New Document, you do not get a spine in the Document Layout palette.

By placing pages side by side in the Document Layout palette you can create multi-page spreads.

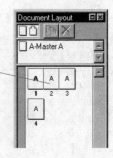

Adding and Deleting Pages

The Document Layout palette provides a convenient, visual method for managing the overall structure of your XPress documents. You can quickly add and delete pages using the palette.

I   To create additional document pages, press and drag the A-Master A icon down into the document pages area of the Document Layout palette. As you do this the A-Master A icon becomes a dotted rectangle with the Pointer cursor inside.

If the new page cursor is not showing when you release the mouse you do not get a new page.

2   Position the dotted rectangle to the right of A1, below A1, and to the left of the spine in a 'Facing Pages' document, and the Pointer cursor becomes a New Page cursor when you are in an acceptable position to create a new page.

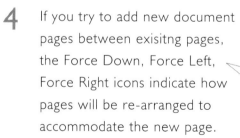

Save your document before adding pages, especially if you are working in a Facing Pages document and you already have contents on pages. When you add pages to a Facing Pages document XPress repositions, renumbers and reformats pages, if necessary, so that they conform to their left and right masters.

3   Release. A new page icon appears in the palette – A2. The margin, column (etc) settings for this page are based on those of the A-Master A page.

4   If you try to add new document pages between exisitng pages, the Force Down, Force Left, Force Right icons indicate how pages will be re-arranged to accommodate the new page.

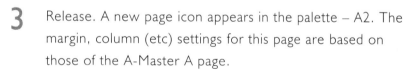
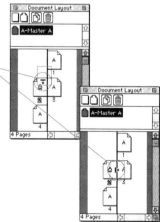

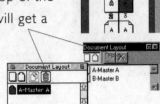

5 To delete a document page, click once on the Page Icon to highlight it.

6 Click on the Delete Icon at the top of the Document Layout palette. You will get a warning message checking that you really do wish to delete the page, including all items on it.

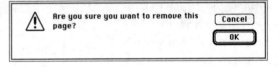

HANDY TIP

To delete multiple pages, select a page, then hold down Shift and click on another page icon to specify a consecutive range of pages. To select non-consecutive pages, select a page, then hold down Command/Ctrl and click to select additional pages.

7 Click OK if you want to continue and delete the page.

⚠ Are you sure you want to remove this page?   Cancel   OK

Moving through a Document

You can use the Document Layout Palette or commands in the Page menu to move through your document.

1. To move to a new page double-click the appropriate page icon in the Document Layout palette. Notice that the Page Number indicator in the bottom left corner of your QuarkXPress window indicates which page you are on.

An emboldened page number in the Document Layout palette indicates the page currently showing in the document window.

2. To move through a document using the Page menu, choose the Page menu, then select from Previous, Next, First or Last.

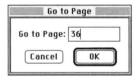

3. To specify a page you want to move to, choose Page > Go to (Command/Ctrl+J). Enter the page number you want to move to. Click OK. This is particularly useful in long documents.

4. Press and hold on the Page Indicator pop-up and select a page to move to.

Using the Page Menu

You can also add and delete document pages using options in the Page menu. The Page menu options are particularly useful when you need to add or delete more than just a few pages.

1 To add document pages choose Page > Insert. The Insert pages dialogue box appears.

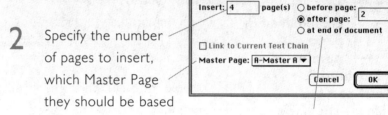

2 Specify the number of pages to insert, which Master Page they should be based upon and where in relation to existing pages you want the new pages inserted. OK the dialogue box.

3 To delete document pages, choose Page > Delete. The Delete Pages dialogue box appears.

You do not get a Warning message allowing you to change your mind when you use the Delete pages dialogue box.

4 Specify the range of pages you wish to delete. OK the dialogue box

Master Pages

Create, position and format items on a master page exactly as you do when working on a document page.

Master Pages are fundamental to working efficiently in most long documents and they are essential when you want elements such as page numbering, dateline, guides and so on to be repeated consistently on document pages.

When you add document pages they will automatically include the items set up on the Master Page on which they are based. You can edit and delete master page items on document pages.

Before you can create the various elements of your Master Page, or if you want to change the Master Guides, you must first move to the Master Page.

If you have more than one master page in the document you can use the same techniques to move to the ß-Master ß and so on.

1 If the Document Layout palette is showing simply double-click the A-Master A icon.

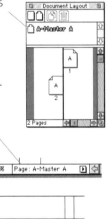

2 You can verify that you have moved to a master page by checking the page number indicator in the bottom left corner of the XPress document window. Also, at the top left corner of each Master Page there is a chain or broken chain icon (depending on whether or not you selected the automatic text box option in the New Document dialogue box).

3 Alternatively, choose Page > Display > A-Master A.

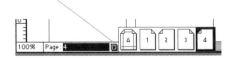

4 Or, use the pop-up in the Page Number indicator to choose the A-Master A icon.

Automatic Page Numbering

For long documents especially, use automatic page numbering when you do not want to number pages manually. Automatic page numbering is set up on a Master Page.

1   Move to a Master Page. Create a text box where you want the page numbers to appear.

2   Make sure you have the Content tool selected. Hold down Command/Ctrl then type the number 3 on the keyboard. The automatic numbering symbol appears in the text box. If you now move to a document page you will see that it is numbered according to its position in the document.

3   The automatic page number symbol is a text character, so you can highlight it and apply formatting as required. All page numbers on document pages will have this formatting applied.

4   If you are working in a Facing Pages document, remember to set up automatic page numbering on both left and right master pages.

Adding and Deleting Master Pages

For more complex documents such as books and magazines you often need more than one Master Page. For example, for a magazine you might want a three column grid for features pages and a four column grid for news pages.

You can create new Master Pages by copying an existing master with all its settings and formatting, or you can work on a fresh, completely blank master page.

When you create a new Master Page you do not automatically move to that Master Page. Make sure you move to the appropriate Master Page before you change Master Guides or edit Master Page items.

1 To copy an existing Master Page layout, click on the Master Page you want to copy to select it. Then click the Duplicate Master Page icon. A new Master Page icon appears in the Document Layout palette. New Master Pages are added in alphabetical order. The new Master Page is an exact replica of the original.

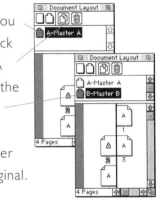

2 Choose Page > Master Guides if you want to make changes to the number of columns, and margin guides for the currently active Master Page.

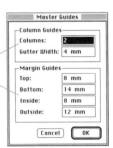

3 Add, delete or modify Master Page items as necessary.

4 To re-name a Master Page, click on the existing name to highlight it, then type in a new name. The name can start with up to three characters followed by a hyphen, then the new name. The three characters preceeding the hyphen appear in the page icons in the document layout palette.

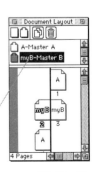

5 To delete a Master Page, click on it to highlight it, then click the Wastebasket/Delete icon.

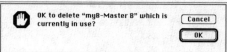

6 If you try to delete a Master Page that is used by document pages you get a warning asking if you want to delete the Master Page. OK the message to remove the Master Page. Any document pages to which the master was applied revert to being based on the blank master. The master page items that appeared on the document pages are deleted or retained, depending on the Master Page Items option in the Document Preferences (see Applying Masters on the next page.)

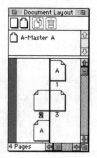

7 Drag the Single Sided blank master icon, or the Facing Pages blank master icon into the Master Pages area of the palette to create a new blank master. The blank masters conform to the original page size, margin, column and gutter settings for the document.

Applying Master Pages

There are times when you need a page to be based on a different master to the one on which it is currently based. This is straightforward if the pages do not have any content and you haven't made changes to any of the Master Page items. It becomes more problematic when you already have contents and/or have made changes to Master Page items.

HANDY TIP

To apply a master page to multiple document pages, use Shift+Click to select a range of document pages, then hold down alt/ option (Mac) Alt (Windows) and click on a Master Page icon to apply the Master Page.

1 To apply a different master to a document page, drag the Master icon you want to convert to, from the Master Page area, onto the page you want to convert. Release when the page you want to convert highlights.

XPress then compares the document page to its previously applied master, deletes any unmodified master items and applies the new master.

Modified items (items you have moved, resized or edited) are retained or deleted depending on the setting for Master Page Items in General Preferences.

2 To specify what happens to modified master items when you apply a different Master Page, choose Edit > Preferences > Document. Click the General tab.

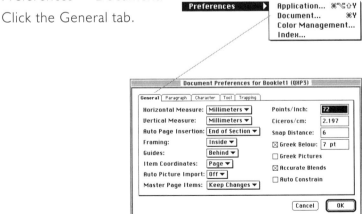

3 From the Master Page Items pop-up, choose Keep
Changes if you want XPress to
keep and not delete modifed
master elements on the
document pages.

| Master Page Items: | ✓ Keep Changes |
| | Delete Changes |

4 Choose Delete Changes if you want XPress to delete both
unmodifed and modifed Master Page items.

Paragraph & Character Styles

A Paragraph Style sheet allows you to set up a description for paragraphs that specifies Character and Paragraph formatting. Once the style is set up, it can be applied wherever necessary in the document. This technique speeds up the formatting of text dramatically and enables you to maintain consistency throughout a document, and from document to document.

Character Style sheets obey the same principles as Paragraph Style sheets, but specify the formatting of individual letters, words, phrases or sentences that do not constitute whole paragraphs.

Covers

Chapter Eleven

Creating Character Style Sheets

Character Style Sheets are useful when you want to apply specific formatting to individual characters, words or phrases on a consistent basis throughout a publication. Character Style Sheets can be applied in combination with Paragraph Style Sheets.

1 To create a Character Style Sheet, choose Edit > Style Sheets (Shift+F11). Choose Character from the New pop-up menu.

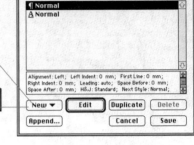

To display the Style Sheets palette, choose File > Show Style Sheets. When you first display the palette the default entries are No Style and Normal. The palette becomes active when you click into a text box with the Content tool selected.

2 Enter a name for the Style Sheet. (Optional) Enter a Keyboard Equivalent. This is a number that you must enter using the number keypad to the right of your keyboard. You do not have to enter a Keyboard Equivalent, but they provide a quick and effective method for applying Style Sheets to selected text.

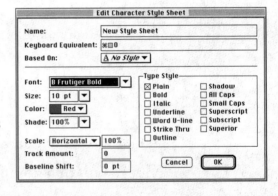

3 Create the Settings you want for Font, Size etc. (see Chapter 4 for details on setting Character Attributes).

...cont'd

4 Click OK in the Edit Character Style Sheet dialogue box. Click the Save button in the Style Sheets for ... dialogue box.

Close all document windows, then create Character and Paragraph Style Sheets if you want the Style Sheets to appear as default Style Sheets for all subsequently created documents. Style Sheets created when a document is active are specific to that document.

5 The new style appears in the Character Style Sheets area of the Style Sheets palette.

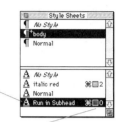

6 If you entered a Keyboard Equivalent, this is indicated to the right of the Style Sheet name in the palette.

Creating Paragraph Style Sheets

BEWARE

Each Paragraph Style Sheet you create must have a default Character Style Sheet associated with it. For this reason it is worth setting up one or more Character Style Sheets before you begin creating Paragraph Style Sheets.

A Paragraph Style Sheet controls the formatting of entire paragraphs. They are useful for any paragraph formatting that is used more than once in a document.

1 To create a Paragraph Style Sheet, choose Edit > Style Sheets. Use the New pop-up to choose Paragraph.

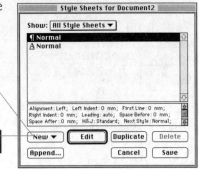

2 Enter a name for the Style Sheet. Enter a Keyboard Equivalent.

3 To set the Character Attributes for the Style Sheet, either use the Style pop-up to choose from an existing Character Style, or click the New button.

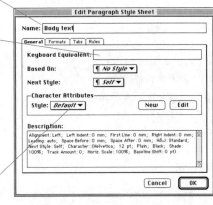

BEWARE

If your text insertion point is flashing in text when you choose Edit > Style Sheets, the settings of this text will be used as the initial settings in the Character (etc) dialogue boxes when you go into them. This can lead to unwanted settings if you are not careful.

4 If you clicked the New button, use the Edit Character Styles dialogue box to create the new Character Style Sheet you want to associate with the Paragraph Style Sheet you are setting up. Click OK in the dialogue box. (See pages 138–139 for details on setting up Character Style Sheets).

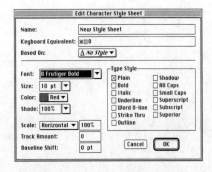

...cont'd

HANDY TIP

Use the Based On pop-up menu when you are creating a Style Sheet, to associate it with another 'base' Style Sheet. When you make changes to the 'base' style, the modification is also applied to any styles based on it.

5 Click the Formats button. Create the settings you want for Paragraph Attributes. (see Chapter 5 for details on setting Paragraph Attributes). Click OK in the dialogue box.

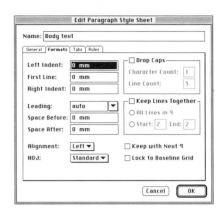

6 Click the Tabs and Rules tabs if you want to specify tabs and paragraph rules as part of your Style Sheet specification. (See Chapter 12 for information on setting tabs and paragraph rules).

7 Click OK in the Edit Paragraph Style Sheet dialogue box. Click the Save button in the Style Sheets for ... dialogue box. If you want to set up another Style Sheet at this stage, instead of clicking on the Save button, use the New pop-up to create another new Style Sheet.

8 When you click the Save button, the new style appears in the Style Sheets palette in the Paragraph Style Sheets area of the palette.

Applying Style Sheets

Use the same basic techniques to apply both Character and Paragraph Style Sheets.

When applying Paragraph and Character Style sheets it is advisable to apply all Paragraph Style Sheets first, then apply Character Style Sheets where necessary.

1 To apply a Paragraph Style Sheet, either click on it to specify one paragraph, or highlight a range of paragraphs.

2 Click on a Paragraph Style in the Style Sheets palette. Or, type the appropriate Keyboard Equivalent on the number Keypad. Alternatively, choose Style > Paragraph Style Sheet and choose a style from the list of available Paragraph Style Sheets.

3 To apply a Character Style Sheet, highlight a range of characters.

4 Click on a Character Style in the Style Sheets palette. Or, type the appropriate Keyboard Equivalent on the number Keypad. Alternatively, choose Style > Character Style Sheets and choose a style from the list of available Character Style Sheets.

5 Use the Style Sheets palette to check which Style Sheets have been applied to text. When the text insertion bar is located in a paragraph to which you have applied a Style Sheet, the name of the Style Sheet is highlighted in the palette.

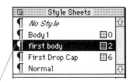

6 You can apply a Character Style Sheet to text that already has a Paragraph Style Sheet applied to it. The Character Style Sheet you apply effectively over-rides the character attributes specified by the Character Style Sheet originally associated with the Paragraph Style Sheet.

7 When the text insertion bar is in text to which both Paragraph and Character Style Sheets have been applied, both styles are highlighted in the Style Sheets palette. The Paragraph style has a small '+' in front of it which indicates that there is an over-ride on the Paragraph Style Sheet.

8 To remove Character Style Sheet formatting and restore the complete paragraph formatting of the style sheet, click on No Style in the Paragraph Styles area of the Palette, then click on the name of the Paragraph Style to re-apply it.

Style Sheets and Local Formatting

You can apply 'local' formatting to text that has already been formatted using Style Sheets.

1 To apply local formatting, highlight a range of text, then use Character and Paragraph Attributes settings to achieve the result you want.

When the text insertion point is within text to which a Style Sheet and local formatting have been applied, it is indicated in the Styles palette by a '+' symbol appearing in front of the Style Sheet name. You get the same effect when you have formatted text manually, and then apply a Style Sheet at a later stage.

You can run into problems with Style Sheets when mixing them with local formatting. You may find that when you apply a different Style Sheet to text with mixed Style Sheet and 'local' formatting, you do not get the formatting you require or expected. The 'local' formatting overrides some of the Style Sheet formatting instructions.

2 To correct a problem caused by mixed Style Sheet and 'local' formatting, click No Style, then click again on the Style Sheet name to re-apply it.

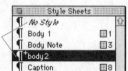

Clicking on No Style does not immediately change the appearance of your text, but it effectively dissociates the selected text from previous 'local' and Style Sheet formatting. When you re-apply the Style Sheet it is no longer affected by any previous formatting over-rides.

Editing Character Style Sheets

When you edit a character style, all the text to which that style is applied is automatically modified according to the change you make.

1 To edit a Character or Paragraph Style Sheet, choose Edit > Style Sheets.

HANDY TIP

Hold down Command/ Ctrl and click on a Style Sheet name in the Styles palette to open the Style Sheets dialogue box.

2 In the Style Sheets for ... dialogue box, use the Show pop-up to control which set of Style Sheets appear in the scroll/display list.

> ✓ **All Style Sheets**
> **Paragraph Style Sheets**
> **Character Style Sheets**
> **Style Sheets In Use**
> **Style Sheets Not Used**

3 Click on the Style name you want to edit. For indentification purposes, in the scroll list of Style Sheets, Paragraph Style sheets are preceeded by a paragraph marker; Character Style sheets by an underlined 'A'. Click the Edit button.

HANDY TIP

Position your cursor on a Style Sheet name, then hold down Ctrl (Mac) and click on a Style Sheet name; or click the right mouse button (Windows) to access a pop-up menu. Use the pop-up to edit, delete or copy the style sheet, or to create a new style sheet.

4 Make the required changes in the Edit Character Style Sheet dialogue box. Click the OK button.

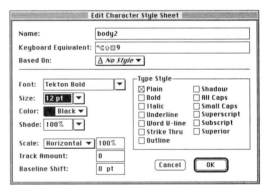

5 Click the Save button in the Style Sheets for ... dialogue box.

Editing Paragraph Style Sheets

REMEMBER

When you edit a Paragraph Style sheet, all paragraphs to which the style is applied are automatically modified according to the changes you make. 'Local' formatting is not affected.

1 To edit a Paragraph Style Sheet, choose Edit > Style Sheets. Select the Paragraph Style in the scroll list. Click the Edit button.

2 Click the General, Formats, Tabs, and Rules tabs, and make changes as required to the various paragraph attributes.

3 Use the Character Attributes Style pop-up if you want to select a different Character Style sheet to associate with the Paragraph Style.

```
Edit Paragraph Style Sheet
Name: body2
General  Formats  Tabs  Rules
Keyboard Equivalent: ⌘⌥⌧9
Based On:           ¶ No Style ▼
Next Style:         ¶ body2 ▼
─Character Attributes─
Style: A body2 ▼        New    Edit

Description:
Alignment: Left;  Left Indent: 0 mm;  First Line: 0 mm;  Right Indent: 0 mm;
Leading: auto;  Space Before: 0 mm;  Space After: 2 mm;  H&J: Standard;
Next Style: body2;  Character: (Name: body2;  Tekton;  10 pt;  Plain;
Black;  Shade: 100%;  Track Amount: 0;  Horiz. Scale: 100%;  Baseline Shift:
0 pt)
                          Cancel    OK
```

4 Click the Edit button if you want to Edit the settings of the Character Style sheet associated with the Paragraph Style Sheet. (Changes you make will also apply to text to which the Character Style sheet has been applied independently of the Paragraph style sheet).

5 Click the New button if you want to create a new Character Style sheet to associate with the Paragraph Style sheet. (See page 138 for instructions on creating Character Style sheets).

6 Click OK in the Edit Paragraph Style Sheet when you are satisfied with your changes. Click the save button in the Style Sheets for ... dialogue box. All paragraphs to which the Style Sheet has been applied are updated to reflect the changes you make.

Appending Style Sheets

To ensure consistency of Style Sheets across documents, and to save yourself from having to recreate the precise specifications for each individual style sheet, you can copy Style Sheet specifications from other XPress documents into the active Xpress document.

HANDY TIP **The techniques for appending style sheets also apply to Colours, H&Js, Dashes and Stripes. Either use the Append button in the specific dialogue boxes, or use File > Append to append settings from more than one category.**

1 To append Character and Paragraph Style Sheets to a document, choose Edit > Style Sheets. Click the Append button.

2 Use standard Macintosh/ Windows directory boxes to locate the XPress

document which has the Style Sheets you want to add to the currently active XPress document. Click on the file name, then click Open.

HANDY TIP **Use Shift+Click to select a consecutive range of Style Sheets; use Command/ Ctrl+Click to select non-consecutive Style Sheets.**

3 To copy an individual Style Sheet, click on its name in the Available scroll list, then click the Add Arrow to add the style to the Include list. Repeat the

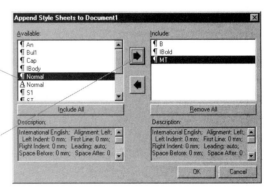

process until you have all the Style Sheets you want to append included in the Include list. Once a Style Sheet is added to the include list, it is removed from the Available list so that you cannot add it twice.

4   Select a Style Sheet name in the Include list, then click the Remove arrow to place the Style Sheet back into the Available list.

5   Click OK in the Append Style Sheets dialogue box. You get a Warning box indicating that any H&Js, Colours, and Dashes and Stripes that are used in the selected Style Sheets will also be appended to the active XPress document. You can select the the 'Don't Show This Warning Again' option to prevent the Warning message appearing in the future.

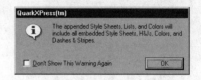

6   Click the Save button in the Style Sheets for ... dialogue box. The Style Sheets are appended to the active XPress document.

Tabs and Rules

Sooner or later you will need to create a table using tabs. Tabs are essential for creating professional, accurately spaced, tabular information. Paragraph Rules might also be used in tables or in running copy, particularly for headings and subheadings.

Covers

Chapter Twelve

Setting Tabs

Use tabs when you want to line up text at precise positions across the page, as in timetables and price lists.

Tabs are treated as a paragraph attribute. If you have the text insertion bar flashing within a paragraph, then use Style > Tabs; you are setting tabs specifically for that paragraph. Highlight a range of paragraphs if you want to set or edit tabs for more than one paragraph at a time.

When you begin working with tabs it is probably least confusing to set tabs in an empty text box, then enter and tab the text across, and finally edit the tab positions if necessary.

1   To set up tabs, make sure you have the Content tool selected and that the text insertion bar is flashing in an empty text box. Choose Style > Tabs.

2   Notice that as well as entering the Tabs dialogue box, a tab ruler is displayed along the top of the active text box. The ruler can be a considerable help when you are estimating a position for a tab. You can also use the ruler to position a tab manually (see below).

3   Choose a Tab alignment by clicking on the appropriate icon. There are tab alignment icons for Left, Right, Centre, Decimal, Comma and Align On.

4 Enter a numeric position for the tab in the position box. A highlighted tab marker appears on the tab ruler above the active text box. Click the Set button. Clicking Set fixes the tab at that position and deselects it. If the tab marker is not deselected, as soon as you enter a new position value, the new value is applied to the still selected tab marker.

Left	Center	Right	Decimal	Comma	Align On

Position:	20 mm	Set
Fill Characters:		Clear All
Align On:		

HANDY TIP

Drag the title bar of the Paragraph Attributes dialogue box to reposition it if necessary to see the tab ruler.

5 Alternatively, you can position tabs manually. Make sure you can see the tab ruler, position your cursor where you want a tab, then click to place the tab. The tab type depends on the alignment icon previously selected.

6 Repeat steps 2–4 until you have the required number of tabs. Click OK in the dialogue box.

BEWARE

The most common initial problem with tabs is text sizes that are too large, leading to entries that don't fit into the available space between the tab stops. The solution – don't put more text between tab stops than will fit.

7 Enter your text in the text box. Type the tab key each time you need to line up text at a particular position.

Apples	200	40p/lb
Peaches	100	65p/lb
Pears	50	50p/lb

Deleting Tabs

You can delete tabs individually, or you can delete all currently set tabs. Deleting all existing tabs can be useful when the tabs have been set in a wordprocessed text file and they are not relevant to your needs in QuarkXPress.

1   To delete all tabs for the selected text, choose Style > Tabs, then click the Clear All button.

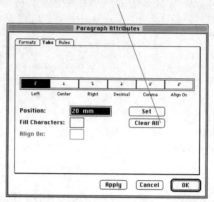

2   To delete a tab manually, position your cursor on a tab marker in the tab ruler, then press and drag it off the tab ruler, and release. Or, click on a tab to highlight it, then press the backspace/delete key.

Editing Tabs

You nearly always need to edit tabs to get your tables to work. Be very careful, before you begin to edit tabs, to highlight the specific range of paragraphs whose tabs you want to change. If you just have your text cursor flashing in an active text box, and you edit tabs, you will not edit the tabs for the entire text box – only the paragraph where your cursor is located.

1 To edit tabs, highlight an appropriate range of paragraphs, then choose Style > Tabs.

2 Make sure the tab ruler is visible. If necessary, reposition the Paragraph Attributes dialogue box. Click once on the tab marker you want to change. The marker is highlighted and its numeric position

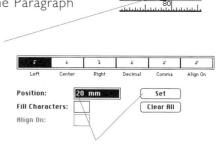

appears in the Position entry field. Enter a new value for the position. Click the Set button to fix the tab at that position and deselect it. Click the Apply button to see the changes applied to any tabbed text in the text box.

3 Alternatively, you can adjust an existing tab marker by dragging it along the tab ruler to a new position. Use the value in the numeric Position entry field as a read out. Release when the tab is in the new position.

4 Repeat steps 2–3 as necessary. Click OK in the dialogue box when you are satisfied.

It can be useful to show invisibles (View > Show Invisibles) when tabbing text so that you can see where you have inserted a tab. This can be especially useful when trying to troubleshoot any problems you might run into using tabs.

Paragraph Rules

Paragraph Rules are extremely useful because they are treated as a paragraph attribute. This means that when you edit text and it reflows, the paragraph rules flow with the paragraphs to which they are applied.

HANDY TIP

Paragraph Rules can be set up as an attribute of a Paragraph Style Sheet.

1 Highlight the paragraph(s) to which you want to apply paragraph rules. Choose Style > Rules. Click the Rule Above/Rule Below box to activate that area. The Rule Above/ Rule Below options are identical.

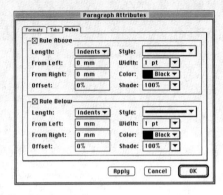

2 Use the Length pop-up to specify the horizontal width of the rule. Provided that you don't have any left or right indents set for the paragraph, and no text inset on the box, choose Indents if you want the rule to extend from the left edge of the box to the right edge.

3 Choose Text if you want the rule to vary in width depending on the amount of text in the paragraph.

4 Enter a From Left/From Right distance to inset the rule from the left and/or right edge of the box or indents.

...cont'd

5 Set an Offset percentage value. This positions the rule vertically. The % value refers to the amount of space between two paragraphs. In this example, 45% of the available space is placed above the rule, 55% below.

6 You can also specify an absolute value in the Offset entry field. Absolute values work form the the baseline of the first line in a paragraph (Rule Above), or the baseline of the last line in a paragraph (Rule Below). To specify an absolute value, enter a number followed by 'pt' for points, 'mm' for millimetres.

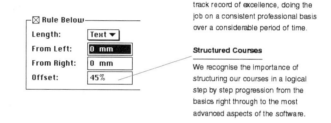

7 Set Style, Width, Colour and Shade values to create the rule you want. Click apply to preview the changes. Click OK in the dialogue box.

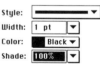

	no. attendess	1	2	3
QuarkXPress	Intro–Adv	250.00	280.00	310.00
QuarkIMMEDIA	Intro–Adv	250.00	280.00	310.00
Adobe Illustrator	Intro–Adv			
Adobe Photoshop	Intro			
Adobe Photoshop	Adv			
Macromedia FreeHand	Intro–Adv			
Adobe PageMaker	Intro–Adv			

	no. attendess	1	2	3
QuarkXPress	Intro–Adv	250.00	280.00	310.00
QuarkIMMEDIA	Intro–Adv	250.00	280.00	310.00
Adobe Illustrator	Intro–Adv	250.00	280.00	310.00
Adobe Photoshop	Intro	250.00	280.00	310.00
Adobe Photoshop	Adv	300.00	340.00	370.00
Macromedia FreeHand	Intro–Adv	250.00	280.00	310.00
Adobe PageMaker	Intro–Adv	250.00	280.00	310.00

Reverse Rules

A reverse rule is a variation on a rule above or below a paragraph, where the text is superimposed on or reversed out of the rule. Reverse Rules are easiest to set up for paragraphs that consist of a single line.

HANDY TIP

Click the apply button each time you make a change in the dialogue box so that you can see how the effect is built up.

REMEMBER

The Width of a rule in QuarkXPress refers to its thickness.

1 To create a reverse rule, select the Content tool, then click into a single line paragraph. Choose Style > Rules. Select the Rule Above option.

2 Specify a width for the rule that is slightly greater than the point size of the text with which you are working.

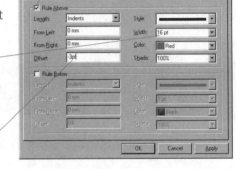

3 Enter a negative offset value in millimetres (type 'mm' after the value), or in points (type 'pt').

4 Use the Colour pop-up to choose a colour for the rule. Specify a tint using the Shade pop-up, or enter a value in the Shade entry field. Click OK in the dialogue box.

REMEMBER

You can colour highlighted text, using the Style > Colour sub-menu, or using the Colour palette.

5 Using the Content tool, highlight the text (which may be difficult to see, depending on the colour of the rule), then choose Style > Character. Use the colour pop-up to choose a colour for the text.

Printing

At various stages as you build your QuarkXPress pages, you will need to print low resolution laser copies from QuarkXPress for basic proofing purposes. XPress pages can also be output to a high resolution image setter when creating separations.

The following section covers printing features necessary for printing low resolution proof copies to a standard laser printer.

Covers

Chapter Thirteen

Copies and Page Range

(Macintosh) Remember to select the appropriate printer in the Chooser before using the File > Print command.

When you print, you can print multiple copies of individual pages, complete documents or any combination of specific pages and page ranges using the Copies and Page Range area of the Print Dialogue.

1 Choose File > Print. Enter the number of copies you want in the Copies field. Specify the page range you want to print. Use a

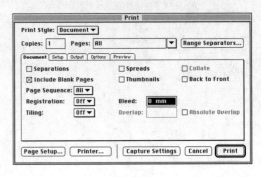

To print a composite proof to a laser printer, make sure you leave the Separations option deselected. A Composite is a printed version of the page where colours are printed on the same page, instead of being separated onto different plates according to their colour breakdown.

comma to specify individual pages, use a hyphen to specify a range of continuous pages. This example would print page 2, followed by pages 4 to 8 and then page 16.

2 Use the Pages pop-up to choose All if you want to print all pages in the publication.

3 Select the Include Blank Pages option if you want blank pages to print.

4 Click the Range Separators button to change the 'comma' and/or 'hyphen' used as range separators in the Pages field to other characters/symbols.

The Copies/ Pages options remain available when any of the Print tabs are selected.

5 Click the Capture Settings button to Save the current printing settings with the document and close the Print dialogue box. The next time you choose File > Print, these settings will appear automatically.

Print – Document Tab

The Document tab is the default tab selected when you choose File > Print.

Spreads are pages arranged horizontally in the document layout palette (see page 126 for further details).

1　Select the Spreads option if you want to print spreads in your document side by side. The paper size you are printing to needs to be large enough to accommodate the spreads to use this option.

2　Select the Thumbnails option to print multiple thumbnail versions of document pages on a single sheet of paper.

3　Select the Back to Front option to print the last page in a document first.

4　The Page Sequence pop-up allows you to specify that only odd or even pages print. You can use this in conjunction with the Back to Front option to print a document on both sides of the paper on some printers.

Page Sequence:	✓ All
	Odd
	Even

5　Select the Collate option when you want to print multiple, collated copies of a multi-page document. This option can increase printing time dramatically, as each copy of the document is printed in its entirety, then the next complete copy is printed, and so on.

6 Select Registration Centred, or Off
Centred for your document pages to

Registration:	✓ Off
	Centered
	Off Center

print with registration and crop
marks. Make sure that the paper size is large enough to
accommodate the additional information. For example, if
the page size of your document is specified as A4, you will
not be able to print Registration marks unless you are
printing to a paper size larger than A4.

7 Use Manual or Automatic tiling
when your document page size is

Tiling:	✓ Off
	Manual
	Automatic

larger than the paper size available
to print on. For example, if you set up an A3 document,
but your printer can only handle A4 pages, Automatic tiling
will print the page on a number of A4 pages in tiles that
can then be assembled for proofing purposes.

Print – Setup Tab

Click the Setup tab to create settings for printer type, paper size, page orientation and scaling.

1 Use the Printer Description pop-up to choose the correct PostScript Printer Description (PPD) for your PostScript printing device. Choosing a PPD automatically provides default values, supplied by the PPD, for Paper Size, Paper Width and Paper Height.

Paper Offset and Page Gap become available when you choose a PPD for an image setter.

2 Use the Paper Size pop-up to choose an appropriate paper size for your printer. Paper Size refers to the actual size of the paper you will print on, not the page dimensions set up in the New Document dialogue box.

3 Enter a value in the Reduce or Enlarge entry field to scale the page to a different size if necessary. Unless you have specific reasons for doing so, leave the Page Positioning unchanged at Left Edge.

4 Click the Portrait or Landscape orientation button to specify the orientation of the printed page.

Print – Output Tab

For low resolution proof copies, click the Output tab to create settings for colour, resolution and halftone screen settings.

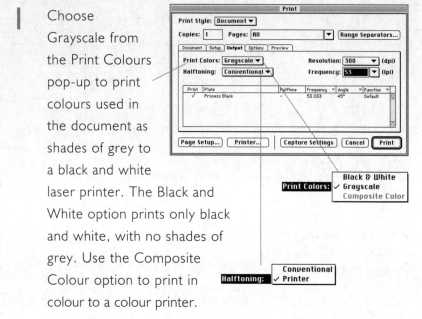

1 Choose Grayscale from the Print Colours pop-up to print colours used in the document as shades of grey to a black and white laser printer. The Black and White option prints only black and white, with no shades of grey. Use the Composite Colour option to print in colour to a colour printer.

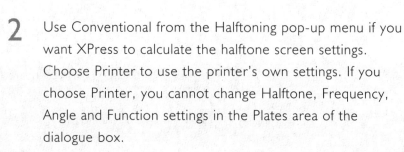

2 Use Conventional from the Halftoning pop-up menu if you want XPress to calculate the halftone screen settings. Choose Printer to use the printer's own settings. If you choose Printer, you cannot change Halftone, Frequency, Angle and Function settings in the Plates area of the dialogue box.

3 If you want to change Resolution and Frequency settings with Conventional as the Halftoning option, enter values as desired.

Print – Options Tab

The most useful options in the Options section of the Print dialogue box are the ones that allow you to control how XPress outputs images.

1 Specify the detail for an image sent to the printer. Normal uses the information held in the original image file that XPress links to (see Picture Usage pages 85–86). Use this option for high resolution output of images. Use Low resolution to print images at screen preview resolution. Use Rough to suppress the printout of placed images and speed up printing time.

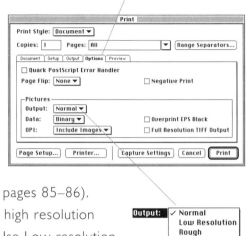

2 Use the Data pop-up to choose from ASCII, Binary and Clean 8-bit. Binary encoded images print faster, but ASCII encoded data is a more portable option, especially on PC networks. Clean 8-bit is a hybrid of ASCII and Binary formats. It is generally more reliable for printing to a parallel port.

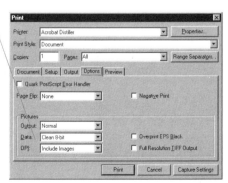

Print – Preview Tab

Use the Preview tab to view the current print settings
before you print the document.

1 The page area icon shows the positioning of a page of the
document in relation to the paper specified. In this
example,
the display
indicates an
output
problem – a
landscape
page set to
print in
portrait
orientation.

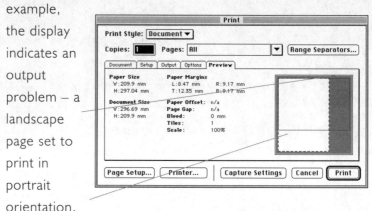

(To correct this, click the Setup tab and change the
orientation to landscape.)

2 The area to the left
of the page icon
displays other
statistical information
about the document.

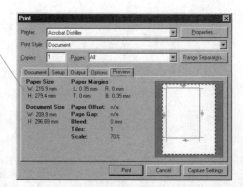

Books, Lists, Indexing

Chapter Fourteen

The Book feature facilitates the production and organisation of long documents such as books and technical manuals, which consist of multiple QuarkXPress documents that need to be worked on as individual documents, yet which must also be consistent in style with the other related chapters.

Lists are most useful for creating automatic tables of content based on text to which specific paragraph style sheets have been applied.

The Index features allow you to create indexes for individual documents, or for a set of QuarkXPress documents set up as a Book.

Covers

The Book Palette

The Book Palette allows you to compile a list of related documents, such as the individual chapters in a book or manual, into a book list. The book list has one Master chapter: settings from it (Style Sheets, H&Js, Colours, Dashes and Stripes) which are used throughout the documents are brought together by the book list to ensure consistency.

REMEMBER

The Master chapter must be imported first so that it assumes the Master status, but it can be moved to a different position in the list at a later stage if necessary.

1   To create a Book file, choose File > New > Book. Use standard Mac/ Windows directory boxes to specify where you want to save the book file. Enter a name. Click the Create button. The Book palette appears.

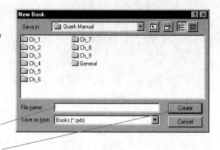

2   Click the Add Chapter button to add the first XPress document to the book list. Use standard directory boxes to navigate to the XPress documents you want to include. Click on a file to select it, then click the Add button. The file is added to the Book list.

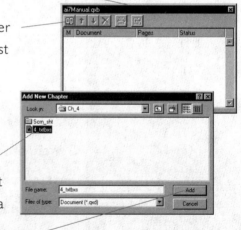

...cont'd

HANDY TIP

It is best to set up a template for your book and use it to start building all the chapters intended to go into the book. This helps ensure consistency of layout, Style Sheets, H&Js (etc) from the outset.

3   The first document you add to the book list becomes the Master chapter for the book, so it is worth setting up and choosing this document very carefully.

The Master chapter is represented in bold.

4   Follow the same process to add further chapters to the book list. The Pages column indicates how pages will be re-numbered when you compile the book.

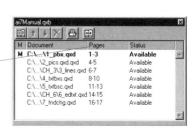

5   To open an existing Book list palette, choose File > Open. Use standard directory boxes to navigate to the file. Click on the book list file to select it, then click Open button.

REMEMBER

Changes, such as adding and deleting, or re-ordering chapters are saved automatically when you close the Book palette, or Quit from XPress.

Managing a Book List

The buttons in the Book list palette allow you to manage the XPress documents in the list.

1 To reorder documents in the list, click on a chapter to select it, then click the Up/ Down arrow buttons as necessary to move the selected chapter to a new position. The page numbering column is updated to reflect the new position of the chapter.

2 To delete a chapter, click on the chapter to select it, then click the Remove button. OK the Warning message.

3 Double-click the chapter name in the palette to open the document. The status changes from Available to Open.

4 To choose a different chapter to be the master, click to the left of the Chapter's name in the Book palette.

Synchronising a Book

When you have compiled and ordered a book list, you are ready to Synchronise the list. When you Synchronise a book list, all Style Sheets, H&Js, Colours, Dashes and Stripes in the documents in the list are made consistent with the settings in the Master document.

If automatic page numbering is set up in the individual documents, the synchronise command will also re-number pages consecutively across the documents in the list.

1 To synchronise a book list, click the Synchronise button.

2 The Warning message indicates that all Style Sheets, Colours, H&Js etc will be modified to match those of the Master chapter, ensuring consistency across all chapters in the book.

3 OK the warning message. XPress proceeds to modify chapters to match the Master chapter.

4 To print the chapters in a Book, click the Print book button. Use the controls in the Print dialogue box to create the settings you want (see Chapter 13 for more information on using the Print dialogue box).

Setting up a List

In order to create a list you must have created and applied style sheets to appropriate paragraphs, such as titles and subheads. When you have created and applied style sheets in a document, you can then use the Edit List dialogue box to gather all instances of text in a particular style into the list.

Lists are particularly useful for automatically generating tables of contents assembled from sets of paragraphs, for example titles or subheads, that have the same paragraph style sheet applied to them.

1 To create a new list, Choose Edit > Lists. The Lists for ... dialogue box appears. Click the New button.

2 Enter a name for the list in the name entry field.

3 Use the Available Styles scroll list to choose the style or styles you want to include in the list. Click on a style to highlight it, then click the right arrow to add it to the list box to the right. You can add more than one style to the list box. (The style no longer appears in the Available Styles list, so you can't include it twice.)

4 To remove a style from the list box, click on it to highlight it, then click the left arrow button. The style is moved back into the Available Styles list.

5 Use the Level pop-up to specify a level for the selected style . The level controls how text is indented in the Lists

...cont'd

It is a good idea to create specific styles sheets for the list before you begin the New List process. In this way the appropriate styles will be available in the Format As pop-up. If you haven't created styles for the list previously, you can choose any style at this stage, build the list, then create and apply appropriate styles when you are ready.

palette. The higher the number the greater the indent. Use higher numbers to visually represent a lower level of priority in the list hierarchy. (See Placing a List on page 172.)

6 The Numbering pop-up controls how the list appears. Text only entries don't have any page numbers after them when the list is generated. Choose - Text ...page#, OR page# ... Text - to specify whether the text part of the list entry appears before or after the page number.

7 Use the Format As pop-up to specify the style sheet you want applied to the text when you build the list.

8 OK the dialogue. The list appears in the scroll box along with any other lists you have created. A description of the highlighted list appears in a scroll box below the main list box. Click the Save button.

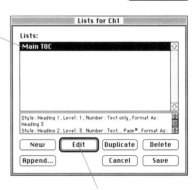

9 To edit an existing list, choose Edit > List. Click on the List you want to edit to select it. Click the Edit button. Use the techniques outlined above to add/delete and reformat styles.

Placing a List

After you have used the List dialogue box to create a list you can then proceed to place the list.

1 Create a new text box and make sure it remains selected. Choose View > Show Lists, to show the Lists palette.

2 Use the List name pop-up to choose the list you want to place if you have created more than one list in the current document. The paragraphs with the appropriate styles applied to them appear in the scroll list, indented according to the indent setting you specified in the Edit List dialogue box.

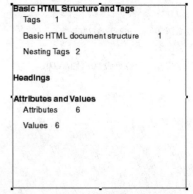

3 The Build button is only available when you have a text box selected. Click the Build button to create the list in the active text box, using the style sheets you assigned in the Edit List dialogue box.

4 Click the Update button if you have made changes in the document that affect the text to which style sheets used by the list have been applied. For example, you may have changed the actual text that is specified to appear in the list, or text included in the list may have reflowed onto a different page. Also click the Update button if you have made changes to the styles included in the list, or to the formatting options of the styles in the list, in the Edit List dialogue box.

REMEMBER

The Build button is only available when there is an active text box in the document.

...cont'd

HANDY TIP

It is best to create a new, empty text box for the list, but XPress will build a list at the text insertion point if necessary.

5 If you have already created the list in the document and you click the Build button, you get a warning message. Click the Replace button to replace the existing list with the current list. Click the Insert button if you want to generate a completely new list.

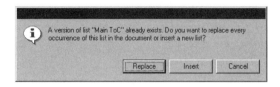

6 Double-click an entry in the List palette to scroll to and display the entry in the QuarkXPress document window.

Creating Index Entries

There are two stages to creating an index. First you set up the index entries, then you build the index. To create index entries you must use the Index palette (View > Show Index).

HANDY TIP

It is a good idea to set up the Character Style Sheet you want to use to format the index entries and the page reference part of index entries before you start to work on creating the index entries.

1   To create a simple, single level index, begin by highlighting a word or phrase you want to appear as an index entry. The word or phrase appears in the Index palette. Leave the Level pop-up on Level 1.

2   Use the Style pop-up to choose a Character Style Sheet to be applied to the page reference part of index entries when you build the index.

BEWARE

The red square brackets around an index entry only appear when the Index palette is showing.

3   Use the Scope pop-up to specify the page number or range that XPress automatically generates for each index entry. Use the Suppress Page # option if you want the index entry to appear in the index without a page number.

HANDY TIP

Click on an existing index entry to highlight it, then click on the Wastebasket/Delete icon to delete the index entry.

4   Click the Add button to add the entry to the scroll list at the bottom of the palette. The highlighted word in the text file is placed in red, sqaure brackets to indicate that it has been indexed.

5   Repeat the above steps to add further entries to the index.

Building an Index

The second stage to creating an index, once you have created the index entries, is building the index. You must have a master page with an automatic text box in order to build an index.

1 Choose Utilities > Build Index.

2 Select the Add Letter Headings option if you want the index to include alphabetic characters to divide the index into sections. Choose a Style Sheet from the pop-up that you want to apply to the alphabetic dividers.

To create an automatic text box in a document that was not initially set up with one, first move to a master page. It can be a good idea to set up a master page specifically for the index (see page 133). Create a text box. Select the Linking tool, click on the Broken Chain icon in the top left corner, then click into the text box to make it an automatic text box.

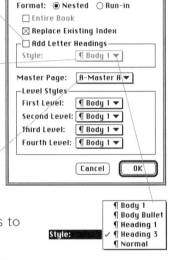

3 Use the Master Page pop-up to specify the master page on which you want the index pages to be based. The master page you specify must contain an automatic text box.

4 To control the appearance of entries in the index, choose a Style Sheet you want to apply to the entries from the First Level pop-up.

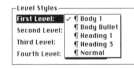

5   Click OK in the dialogue box. XPress automatically generates new pages at the end of the document and flows in a text file composed of the index entries, generating additional pages as necessary to accommodate the index. If you specify a facing page master page, XPress adds a right hand page to begin the index.

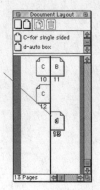

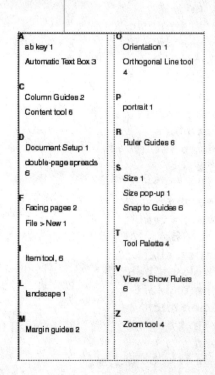

A	O
ab key 1	Orientation 1
Automatic Text Box 3	Orthogonal Line tool 4
C	**P**
Column Guides 2	portrait 1
Content tool 6	
D	**R**
Document Setup 1	Ruler Guides 6
double-page spreads 6	**S**
	Size 1
F	Size pop-up 1
Facing pages 2	Snap to Guides 6
File > New 1	
I	**T**
Item tool, 6	Tool Palette 4
L	**V**
landscape 1	View > Show Rulers 6
M	**Z**
Margin guides 2	Zoom tool 4

Chapter Fifteen

Working with Beziers

When you use any of the range of Bezier tools in QuarkXPress you are creating Bezier paths or curves which define the shape of the resultant picture box, text box or line. The Bezier tools provide a creative flexibility which was previously only found in drawing applications such as Adobe Illustrator and Macromedia FreeHand.

Covers

Drawing Bezier Boxes and Curves

 Bezier Picture Box Tool

 Bezier Text Box Tool

 Bezier Line Tool

The Bezier Picture Box and Text Box tools and the Bezier Line tool work in an identical manner, except that the box drawing tools create closed boxes that can be filled with text, an image or colour. The Bezier Line tool creates open paths or lines.

1   To create a Bezier box, select either the Bezier Text Box or Picture Box tool and position your cursor on the page where you want to start drawing the shape.

2   Press and drag. This sets the position of the first point. The curve handle that you drag out will control the length and direction of the curve that will leave the first point.

3   Release the mouse button. Move the cursor to a new position. (Do not press and drag the mouse). The new position of the cursor will become the position of the next point.

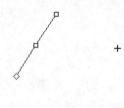

HANDY TIP

To create straight line segments between points, simply move the cursor then click instead of pressing and dragging.

4   Press and drag. This sets the second point.

5   The curve handle that you drag out will control the length and direction of the next curve segment if you create another point.

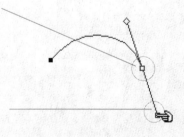

6   Continue the above process: move the cursor, press and drag to set the curve between the point you are setting the preceding point, and to start to define the length and shape of the curve that will leave the point.

7   To close a box, position the cursor on the start point. The cursor changes to a hollow square. Click on the point, or press and drag. You now have a completed, closed box. You can also close a box by double-clicking after you have created the second point.

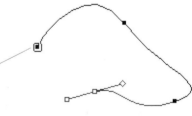

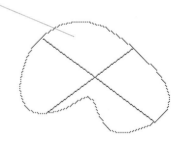

REMEMBER

The length and shape of a curve segment is controlled by the curve handles associated with the points at each end of the curve segment.

Freehand Boxes and Lines

 Freehand Bezier
Picture Box Tool

 Freehand Bezier
Text Box Tool

 Freehand Text
Path Tool

 Freehand Line
Tool

The Freehand Picture box, Text box and Line tools work in an identical manner, except that the two box drawing tools create closed boxes that can be filled with text, an image or colour. The Freehand Line tool creates open paths or lines.

1 To create a Freehand Picture or Text box, select the appropriate tool from the Picture box or Text box tool group.

2 Position your cursor on the page. Press and drag. The shape of the box is set as you drag the mouse.

3 When you position your cursor at the start point, the small square cursor indicates that you will complete the box and join up the start and end point when you release.

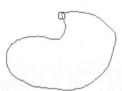

 BEWARE

You cannot create a closed path or box using the FreeHand line tool.

4 If you release before you return to the start point, XPress draws a straight line segment between the end and start points to create a closed shape or box.

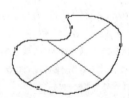

 HANDY TIP

To move a freehand line, position your cursor on a line. The cursor changes to the bezier editing cursor. Hold down Command/Ctrl and use the Item or Content tool to move a selected freehand line without editing its shape.

5 To draw a Freehand Line, select the Freehand Line tool. Position your cursor on the page, then press and drag. The freehand path is created as you drag the mouse. Points are set to define the shape of the path when you release the mouse.

Bezier Terminology

Bezier boxes and lines consist of two or more points joined by curve or straight line segments. You can edit points, curve and line segments and you can also adjust curve handles which are associated with points. Being able to identify exactly what you have selected is essential for working effectively with Beziers.

Paths

A Path consists of a series of points, joined by curve segments or straight line segments.

Paths can be open or closed. You create closed paths – picture or text boxes drawn with the Bezier Text and Picture box drawing tools – when you click back at the point from which you started drawing the box.

You create open paths with the Bezier Line and the Freehand Bezier Line tools, as well as the Bezier and FreeHand Bezier Text Path tools. The start and end points of an open path do not join up.

Points

When you draw with the Bezier drawing tools you set points which, in conjunction with the curve handles, define the shape of the path. Points are joined to each other by curve or straight line segments.

When selected, a Smooth point is indicated by a hollow diamond, Symmetrical points by a hollow square, and Corner points by a hollow triangle.

Curve Handles

Points connecting curve segments have associated curve handles. The curve handles control two aspects of the curve – its length and its direction. Using the Item or Content tool, click on a point to select it. When you select a point, any curve handles associated with the point also appear.

1 Drag a curve handle further away from its point to increase the length of the curve segment. Bring it closer and you decrease the length of the curve.

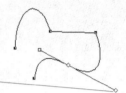

2 Change the angle of the curve handle (by dragging the curve handle in a circular direction) to change the direction of the curve as it enters or leaves the point.

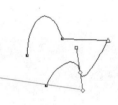

3 A curve segment is typically defined by the position of the outgoing handle of one point and the position of the incoming handle of the next point along.

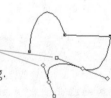

4 Straight line segments do not have associated curve handles.

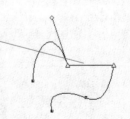

Working with Points and Segments

There are three types of point that you work with in QuarkXPress – Symmetrical, Smooth and Corner. You can convert points from one type to another to suit your needs. You can also convert straight line segments to curve segments and vice versa.

To work with the points, curve and line segments, and curve handles in a Bezier path, the Item > Edit > Shape option must be selected.

1 Symmetrical Points ensure a smooth, continuous curve through the point. When you drag either of the curve handles and change its angle, the opposite curve handle moves to balance it – the two curve handles always remain in alignment. Also, if you increase or decrease the distance of the curve handle from its point, the opposite curve handle changes by the same amount ensuring that both handles remain equidistant from the point.

When selected, Symmetrical points are identified by a hollow square, Smooth points by a hollow diamond, and Corner points by a hollow triangle.

2 A Smooth Point is similar to a Symmetrical point and ensures a smooth, continuous transition or curve from the incoming to the outgoing curve segment. When you change the angle of one curve handle, the other curve handle balances it – maintaining perfect alignment between handles. However, unlike the Symmetrical point, when you increase/decrease the distance of the curve handle from the point, the distance of the opposite handle relative to the point is not adjusted.

3 Corner points are necessary when you want to achieve a sharp change of direction at the point. When you drag a curve handle it moves completely independently of the other curve handle.

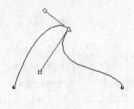

4 To convert from one point type to another, click on a point with either the Item tool or Content tool, to select it. Click on an appropriate point type in the Measurements palette. The icons in the palette represent Symmetrical, Smooth and Corner points.

5 Alternatively, choose Item > Point/ Segment Type and select a different point type from the sub-menu.

6 To convert a straight line segment into a curve segment or vice versa, click on a line segment joining two points, then click the Straight or Curved Segment icon in the Measurements palette. Alternatively, you can choose Item > Point/Segment Type to choose a segment type from the sub-menu.

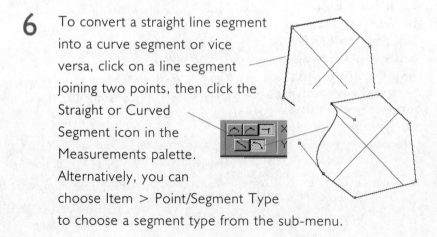

Selecting and Editing Points

Use the following techniques when you need to select and manipulate points to achieve the shapes you want.

You can select points with either the Item tool or Content tool.

1 To select a point, first select a path. The points appear as solid black squares.

To see the points that constitute a path when you click on it, you must have the Item > Edit > Shape option selected. The option is ticked if it is on. If this option is not on, when you click on a shape you get the standard resize handles for the item.

2 Position your cursor on a point – it changes to the Edit point cursor. Click on the point to select it. Depending on the point type, curve handles appear at the point. Press and drag a point to reposition it. Incoming and outgoing curve or straight line segments are adjusted accordingly.

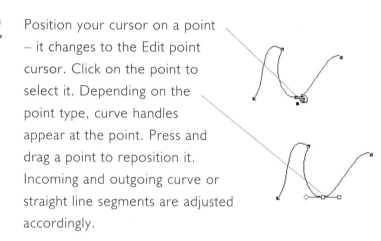

3 Select one point, then hold down Shift and click on other points to select more than one point. Press and drag any one point in a multiple selection to move all the selected points.

You can still edit individual curve handles, even when multiple points are selected.

4 Double-click a point to select all the points in an open or closed path. Press and drag on any of the selected points to move the entire path.

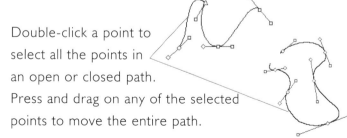

5   To delete a point, make sure the path is selected then position your cursor on the point. Hold down alt/option (Mac) Alt (Windows). The cursor changes to the delete point cursor. Click to delete the point. The path is redrawn without the point.

6   Hold down Control (Mac) Ctrl+Shift (Windows) and click on a point with curve handles to retract the curve handles.

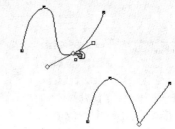

7   Position the cursor on a point without handles, hold down Control (Mac) Ctrl+Shift (Windows), then press and drag off the point to drag out curve handles.

8   To add a point, make sure a path is selected, hold down alt/option (Mac), Alt (Windows), then click on the path.

Index